Advance Praise for *Stress Less, Accomplish More*

"Emily is a deep scholar of meditation. Despite that, she makes learning it incredibly playful, fun, and entertaining. *Stress Less, Accomplish More* is anything but boring, and it very well may change your life."
— Andrew Huberman, Ph.D., Professor of Neurobiology, Stanford University School of Medicine

"I've been working with Olympic athletes and high achievers for over two decades, and I'm picky about the people I refer my clients to. Emily Fletcher sits at the top of my list because her system works. She takes the benefits of meditation to a completely new level, while not scaring away the newbie. Invest in yourself!"
— Todd Herman, performance coach to Olympic athletes and author of *The Alter Ego Effect*

"I truly hope people read and adopt the practice Emily Fletcher teaches so elegantly in *Stress Less, Accomplish More*. The less stress you have in your life, the less stress you will pass on to your children."
— Dr. Shefali Tsabary, author of *The Conscious Parent*

"I've met thousands of proponents of meditation, and Emily Fletcher stands out like a shining star. Her way of teaching, intellect, and charm take the concepts of mindfulness and meditation to new heights. Read this book and study with Emily if you're seeking to bring meditation into your life."
— Vishen Lakhiani, founder and CEO of Mindvalley and *New York Times* bestselling author of *The Code of the Extraordinary Mind*

"Emily Fletcher's praiseworthy Ziva Technique as taught in *Stress Less, Accomplish More* meets each of us precisely where we are in the present moment of our lives, elevating us to our highest potential in our personal and professional creative expressions."
    —Michael Bernard Beckwith, bestselling author and founder of the Agape International Spiritual Center

"I prescribe the meditation Emily teaches in this book to my patients to help them optimize their mental and physical health. We even brought Emily to teach our doctors at Parsley Health. She makes meditation so accessible. Her style is the easiest to adopt into a busy life that I have ever found (and I've tried a lot)."
    —Robin Berzin, M.D., CEO of Parsley Health

"This book has the ingredients for you to accomplish what you didn't think was possible: Fifteen minutes twice a day equals increased productivity, better decision making, and better quality of sleep. It also makes you more mindful, which can have a positive impact on the decisions you make around food, which is good for you and for the world."
    —Gunhild Stordalen, M.D., president of EAT Foundation

"This book is the antidote to today's insane mentality. Emily helps bring sanity to your day and peace to your entire life, . . . all without giving up your dreams and aspirations. It's a great read."
    —Pedram Shojai, O.M.D., *New York Times* bestselling author of *The Urban Monk*

STRESS LESS, ACCOMPLISH MORE

MEDITATION FOR
EXTRAORDINARY PERFORMANCE

EMILY FLETCHER

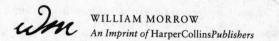

WILLIAM MORROW
An Imprint of HarperCollinsPublishers

For audio exercises from the book and additional bonuses, visit www.zivameditation .com/bookbonus.

HarperCollins books may be purchased for educational, business, or sales promotional use. For information, please email the Special Markets Department at SPsales@ harpercollins.com.

A hardcover edition of this book was published in 2019 by William Morrow, an imprint of HarperCollins Publishers.

FIRST WILLIAM MORROW PAPERBACK EDITION PUBLISHED 2019.

Designed by William Ruoto

Library of Congress Cataloging-in-Publication Data has been applied for.

ISBN 978-0-06-274751-8

21 22 23 24 LSC 10 9 8 7 6 5 4 3 2

This book is dedicated to everyone who has "tried meditation" and felt like a failure.

You are not a meditation failure; you just haven't been taught yet.

This book will teach you.

Contents

Foreword

WHEN I FIRST MET EMILY, WE WERE BOTH LECTURING AT AN event in Greece. She was telling me about her meditation practice, and in the back of my mind I was thinking, *Oh, sure. I studied Zen Buddhism. I've gone on retreats. I've meditated for twelve hours a day. I've also been a yoga teacher and still do yoga all the time. I have plenty of health hacks in my tool kit.* I felt like I already had my stress under control, but I was intrigued by what she had to say.

The more I listened to Emily, the more I realized that she was talking about something else—something deeper, more powerful, and potentially life-changing. What really got my attention was the way she kept talking about doing less while accomplishing more.

Of course, the idea of adding yet another demand on my time—even just fifteen minutes twice a day—seemed crazy. Life keeps me extremely busy: In addition to being a practicing physician, author, and parent, I give lectures and am a regular medical contributor on many television shows. Squeezing more into my daily schedule seemed impossible.

But Emily made a compelling case. I agreed to try meditating with her while we were in Greece, and I was shocked when I realized just how different this form of meditation felt from what I had done in the past. I decided to take the Ziva Meditation training with her, and afterward, I began to sleep better almost right away, but that was only a small part of the benefit. My mind felt clearer; my focus sharpened, and I even started having more time in my day! I didn't notice I had been anxious or stressed—until I wasn't!

I was intrigued enough by the results to commit to at least another month, just to see what would happen.

To say I was shocked by what Emily's style of meditation did for me is an understatement. I didn't realize I was stressed and anxious; I didn't think I was agitated. And I was already achieving at a high level. But after just two months, I felt happier, calmer, and less anxious. I have so much more energy. Now if I don't sleep well, I can do the Ziva Technique and feel as refreshed as if I've just had a long nap. I used to get tired at the end of the day, but now I get a new surge of energy after my second sitting and feel able to go out at night and have fun. For the few minutes I put into meditation each day, I get back at least an extra three hours of focus and quality work. The benefits of meditation bleed into everything I do.

Maybe the most surprising aspect of Emily's approach is how easy and accessible it is. This is the kind of meditation you can do anytime, anywhere. You don't have to clear your mind, burn incense, or be alone in the forest. I've meditated in conference rooms, in parking lots, on airplanes—you name it. When I tell my patients about Ziva, I say, "You don't realize how stress may be impacting your performance until you start feeling better. And you can't believe how much more you're capable of until you try this out."

I encourage everyone to check out the Ziva Technique. I can honestly say I can't live without it. Now I don't have time *not* to meditate.

"Stress less, accomplish more." It's for real, trust me.

—Mark Hyman, M.D.
Director of the Cleveland Clinic Center for Functional Medicine and author of *Food: What the Heck Should I Eat?* and eleven other bestselling books

Preface

AS A NEUROSCIENTIST WHO IS ALSO INTERESTED IN "WELL-
ness" (the modern, less shame-inspiring replacement term for "self-
help"), I sit at an interesting, albeit somewhat uncomfortable, vantage
point. On one hand, I see a new and exciting era emerging, in which
science is getting leveraged toward the development of truly useful
practices for enhancing people's lives. On the other hand, I also see a
lot of misuse of the word *science* as a marketing tool to sell everything
from supplements to esoteric breathing practices to brain-machine-
interface devices. To be clear: There are some very interesting, even
powerful tools emerging in all corners of the wellness arena, but most
lack the essential components that I, personally, would want to see
before dedicating my time, energy, and money to them.

Those criteria are:

1. Deep descriptive rigor. I need to know what is involved in
   the practice.
2. Predictive power. I need to know what I can reasonably
   expect during and after.
3. Actionable. I need a clear description of what to do, when
   to do it, and how.
4. Moves the needle. The results need to make a big, positive
   difference.

All that might seem like a tall order, but I believe it is reasonable to ask for that from the self-designated teachers, coaches, gurus, and web personalities who hock this stuff. So when I heard that someone named Emily Fletcher was giving a talk on meditation at a conference I was attending, I figured I would skip it. Another American "yogi"—seen that one before. Fortunately for me, the Internet connection worked only from inside the conference room, so I decided to handle e-mail in there while Emily spoke on the stage.

Looking back, I'm so grateful I made that choice. I think it was Emily's words—"These neuroscientists are catching up to what meditators have known for thousands of years: that meditation actually makes our brains better!"—that got my attention. After all, she was basically taking a jab at me. But as I listened further, I realized, *This woman really gets it.* First off, Emily possesses the unique skill of being able to make something as "tranquil" as meditation truly exciting, while at the same time grounding it in both its ancient roots and real modern scientific inquiry. She knows the classic jargon, but she isn't afraid to assign user-friendly definitions to the various terms surrounding meditation and mindfulness practices. I find this incredibly useful. For example, nowadays the word *meditation* seems to be used as a catchall for any eyes-closed activity besides sleep or coma, and *mindfulness* is even less well-defined. Emily has a different, far more organized take on all this. In *Stress Less, Accomplish More,* she educates you: Mindfulness is really about the now, whereas meditation is about letting go of stress from the past. She even defines *manifesting* (a word I'd frankly never been comfortable with) as a set of actionable steps. Whether everyone agrees on these definitions is less important than the fact that by putting them out there, Emily breaks down the major barrier to getting *you* into a daily practice.

Stress Less, Accomplish More beautifully establishes a *why* to each step. All the incredible benefits of engaging in a regular meditation practice that people tout—better sleep, calmer state of mind, less reactivity, better sex, and so on—still exist, but in *Stress Less, Accomplish More,* Emily teaches you what to expect *during the actual practice itself.* That is a unique and powerful gift, and no, it doesn't require that you spend ten days sitting in silence. It is about small, actionable, daily steps to achieve large, specific benefits. And she teaches you how.

So now, three years after hearing Emily speak and learning the Ziva Technique, I have come to realize that I was fundamentally wrong: Emily is not just another American who spent some time in India, picked up some lingo, did some stretches, and came back to the United States to tell us about it. Emily is a deep scholar of meditation, and is clarifying what both ancient and modern meditation really is, how it works, and, most important, what it can do for you. *Stress Less, Accomplish More* brings together the very best of what is possible in terms of educating you on meditation (my criterion #1 above), what you can expect at each stage (#2), how to do it (#3), and some of the many incredible benefits it can create (#4). Somehow (perhaps it is her Broadway training?) Emily also makes this process incredibly playful, fun, and entertaining. That wasn't on my list of criteria, but perhaps it should be #5, because as you'll soon discover, *Stress Less, Accomplish More* is anything but boring, and it very well may change your life.

—Andrew Huberman, Ph.D.

Professor of Neurobiology, Stanford University School of Medicine

Introduction

YOU MAY BE THINKING, *ME? MEDITATION?* THAT'S WHAT I thought, too. A youth spent in the Florida Panhandle doesn't really provide the best opportunity to come in contact with any sort of meditation. I competed in beauty contests, sang the national anthem at the opening of a Walmart Supercenter, and went to a lot of keg parties. But meditation? It never even came up.

By the age of twenty-seven, I was performing on Broadway in the show *A Chorus Line,* understudying three of the lead roles. Acting on Broadway was a childhood dream, but the reality had become a nightmare. If my performance was off, I was devastated. My anxiety kept intensifying, I had terrible insomnia, and I started to go gray—at the tender age of twenty-seven. I was constantly getting sick or injured. There I was, living my dream—doing the one thing I had wanted to do since I was nine years old—and I was miserable. Broadway was supposed to be sunshine, roses, and martinis with Liza. Instead, my experience of the Great White Way was splitting rooms in overpriced apartments, eating tuna fish out of a can, and complaining about my bunions.

One day I was in the dressing room watching another actress named Deonne. She was understudying five leads, but unlike me, she was completely calm and centered; she was effervescent and a pleasure to be around. Every song she sang was a celebration. Every dance she did was full of joy. Even every bite of food she ate, she cherished. I asked her how she pulled it off, and her answer was, "I meditate."

I promptly rolled my eyes at her answer and brushed it off as impossible. There was nowhere near the neuroscience then that there is now, so it was hard for me to understand how something like meditation could be impacting her performance so dramatically. But I kept feeling worse—I hadn't slept through the night in more than a year and a half, which was severely impacting my performance. I finally felt so embarrassed about my ability to perform that I knew I had to do something. Deonne mentioned that her meditation teacher was in town and asked me to come along to an intro talk. Everything the teacher said made sense to me; it rang true. I signed up for the course. After only the first two hours of training, I was "meditating"—meaning I was in a different state of consciousness from what I had ever been in before—and I actually liked it!

That night I slept soundly for the first time in eighteen months. That was over a decade ago, and I haven't had insomnia since. I stopped getting sick, I stopped going gray—in fact, my hair color came back. Best of all, I began enjoying my job again. And I got much better at it. I stopped seeking validation and approval from the audience, which paradoxically made me a much better performer. I was always ready, and I could finally hit the stage with calmness and confidence. That naturally led me to think, *Wait a minute—why doesn't everyone do this?*

That's when I became inspired to teach meditation. I quit Broadway and traveled to India, where I began what became a three-year teacher-training process. No, I was not in India that whole time. I am not that hard core. This ended up being the most creative, rewarding thing I've ever done. When I tell my story, people always ask how I could walk away from a successful career and take the risk of starting Ziva Meditation. The simple answer is that my life goals became much clearer when I began meditating daily, and I tapped into energy and insight that I'd never before realized I had. This book is about giving you, the reader, access to this insanely powerful tool. You can find that same inner-connectedness that my more than twelve thousand students and I access twice daily. You'll learn how to improve your performance by removing stress, boosting energy, increasing drive, and ultimately how to become more successful at life in the process.

» This Is Not Your Typical Meditation Book

Before we go any further, I want to clarify something. This is not another meditation book heralding the benefits of higher states of consciousness without giving you any real tools to get there. This book is all about extraordinary performance. And I don't just mean for artistic performers or people on a stage. This book will help you upgrade your personal and professional performance no matter your occupation. It will give you not only an intellectual understanding of how stress may be keeping you from your full performance capabilities, but more important, this book will give you practical tools you can start to use on a daily basis to eradicate that stress and start to up-level your brain, your body, and ultimately your life.

In the following pages, I will train you in a specific technique that you'll be able to do on your own. It's called the Z Technique; it's an adaptation of what I teach live at our studio in New York City and online through our fifteen-day virtual training, zivaONLINE, and it's designed to help you in work and in life. The steps outlined here are specifically created for achievement-minded individuals who are committed to performance enhancement and excellence. Whether you spend your time closing deals or opening sippy cups, the Z Technique will give you a mental edge to help innovate and adapt at the rate that technology demands. By investing in yourself for fifteen minutes twice a day, you can drastically change your outlook and your output in life. In addition to teaching you a daily practice, many of the chapters have exercises at the end that you can use for specific life challenges and to help you gauge your success along the way.

Maybe you've noticed how meditation has quickly transitioned from being a fringe activity to becoming standard practice in the boardrooms of corporate America, and you're curious as to why. Maybe you've tried meditation in the past but gave up because you felt like you could never quite clear your mind, or because you struggled to fit it into your fast-paced life. Or maybe you aren't interested in the practice of meditation at all, but you *are* interested in any tool that can enhance your productivity and performance while decreasing stress.

Whatever the case, you've come to the right place. *Stress Less, Accomplish More* is designed to serve as an introduction to not only meditation but also the three mental tools that make up the Ziva Technique: Mindfulness, Meditation, and Manifesting. This book will give you an explanation of what they are and the science behind how they function as tools for high performers to improve their cognitive function and creativity, while simultaneously releasing stress and improving overall mental and physical health.

There are currently more than six thousand peer-reviewed scientific studies on meditation. In the following pages, I will share the most exciting ones with you, including some from Harvard Medical School, Stanford, and Wake Forest University, and translate how these recent findings apply to your busy life. The findings in these studies range from medically verifiable physical benefits to new scientific analyses that point to the neurological advantages of meditation in mental acuity. All the findings confirm what I have witnessed firsthand with my students, and what you can experience if you read this book and put into practice the techniques you will learn in the coming pages: Meditation can give you deeper and more refreshing sleep and increased energy during the day; make you feel more connected, less anxious, and more level-headed in demanding situations; help you experience better relationships; and even have better sex! One of my students likened meditation to putting on reading glasses she never knew she needed: Suddenly, life comes into sharp focus.

Many of my students have attempted meditation in the past but gave it up for a variety of reasons. Using the Ziva Technique, these same people have been able to reclaim their meditation goals without the guilt of past failures or the confines of a highly rigid system or community. My aim is to rid the world of ex-meditators. By this I mean my goal is to give people who previously felt like meditation failures—for being "too busy" or not being able to "clear their minds"—the knowledge they need to accurately gauge their success and a practice that will actually feel worth the time investment. As we progress through the book, I will guide you as you create a self-sufficient practice that can be easily integrated into even the most demanding schedule. No need for apps, earbuds, crystals, incense, or kaftans. As I mentioned, the Z Technique is a gentler version of the Ziva Technique that I teach live and online; it is a painless way to condition your body and mind for better performance. Whether this is your first time dipping your toe into the meditation pool or you've been doing this for years, *Stress Less, Accomplish More* is both the perfect starting point *and* a refresher course for realizing your full potential. If you have previously been allergic to the word *meditation*, don't call this meditation—just try the Z Technique and see how you feel. If you've had a meditation practice for years but find it a bit too rigid or aren't seeing the return on time investment you would like, try the Z Technique and see if you feel a difference.

It doesn't matter what your profession, ambition, religion, expertise, or experience is. Meditation is simply a tool to help you reach your goals; it's never the goal itself. The main point is this: *We meditate to get good at life, not to get good at meditation.*

If you want to elevate your performance—to eliminate the effects of stress, improve your mental energy, increase your physical health, expand your creativity, and hone your intuition—you've come to the right place. All it takes is the desire to up-level your life and fifteen minutes twice a day. Are you ready to invest in yourself?

WHY MEDITATE?

"I CAN'T MEDITATE."

This is the most common refrain I hear from would-be meditators. For some, "I can't meditate" means "I want to meditate, but seriously, have you seen my schedule?" For others, "I can't meditate" is far more literal: "I tried to meditate, but I couldn't stop my mind from thinking."

Both types of people are usually very sincere in their desire to practice meditation. Both types of people believe meditation is not a viable option for them. And both types of people are wrong.

The disconnect comes from a cultural misunderstanding of the term *meditation*. I think there's one dude out there telling people that in order to meditate, you have to clear your mind. I wish I could find this guy and teach him how to meditate. While it *is* possible to access different states of consciousness, and humans are the only species that can do this at will, the point of meditation is not to clear the mind. I would argue that the "point" of meditation is to get good at life. So if you've ever tried meditation and felt frustrated because you couldn't stop all those crazy thoughts, here's some really good news: The mind thinks involuntarily, just like the heart beats involuntarily. One more time, for dramatic effect: *The mind thinks involuntarily, just like the heart beats involuntarily.* Just for kicks, take two seconds and try to give your heart a command to stop beating.

If you're still reading this, I'll assume you weren't successful. It's easy for us to see that trying to stop the heart from beating is fruitless, yet we continue to try to stop the mind from thinking. Then we feel like a meditation failure and we quit. Who wants to keep doing something that makes you feel as if you're constantly failing? People who find one type of meditation unfulfilling, too time-consuming, or too difficult often reject anything that goes by the same name. The beauty of the Z Technique, however, is that it's almost completely fail-proof—and it's a tool that will help raise your performance in all areas of your life. This style of meditation is so simple that you actually have to *try* to screw it up. Combine that ease with the fact that meditation has been scientifically proven to improve nearly every area of your life without taking away your competitive edge, and I feel confident that you're going to become a meditator (or an ex-ex-meditator, if we want to be really confusing), too. Once you have a technique that is designed for you and a bit of training on how properly to gauge your success, meditation can become an enjoyable part of your daily routine.

But here's the rub: The word *meditation* has become like the word *food*. Blueberries, hot dogs, sushi, potato chips—they're all food, but they all do wildly different things to your body. Similarly, there are hundreds of different styles of meditation, but Westerners tend to pile all the techniques under one umbrella term, even though these varying techniques do vastly different things to your brain and body.

Saying you don't like meditation is like saying you don't like food. Imagine going to a restaurant, looking at your server, and just ordering "food." What's the server supposed to do with that?

Meditation can be broken into a number of different styles: mindfulness, Zen, self-induced transcendence, Vipassana, Kundalini—just to name a few. Some schools of thought identify as few as five different forms; others break it down into more than twenty. For the purposes of this book, we will classify meditation into three main categories, or what I like to call the 3 M's: Mindfulness, Meditation, and Manifesting. Just as eating a hamburger does different things to your body than drinking a chia seed smoothie, different styles of meditation light up different parts of the brain and require different degrees of effort and time. They can also have varying degrees of effectiveness on your performance off the proverbial cushion.

» So Which Style of Meditation Should I Practice?

This is a very personal question, and one you'll ultimately have to answer for yourself. I want to do everything in my power to give you the information you need to make an educated decision based on data and your own personal experience. In this book, I will be referring to two different techniques quite a lot: (1) The Ziva Technique, which is what I teach in person, and in our virtual course, zivaONLINE; and (2) The Z Technique, which, to reiterate, is an adaptation of the Ziva Technique. The Z Technique combines the same beautiful trifecta of Mindfulness, Meditation, and Manifesting, but in a gentler and more universal approach, since I am not able to deliver personal mantras or offer individualized training and guidance the way I can when working with students face-to-face.

To start, let's get crystal clear on the differences between the 3 M's that you will be learning in the coming pages. We'll begin with the first two: mindfulness and meditation. Many people think these are the same, and even use the words as synonyms. This is problematic, especially as both practices are gaining popularity. One mental technique was originally designed for monks, and the other for people with busy minds and busy lives. With meditation becoming increasingly more mainstream, it will be helpful to be well versed on the differences between the two, and to develop a specificity of vocabulary so you don't feel unnecessarily confused or frustrated.

Mindfulness is a "directed focus" mental practice, meaning that you have some point of concentration during the exercise. I would define it as the art of bringing your awareness into the present moment, and it is very effective at handling your stress in the right now.

MINDFULNESS: The art of bringing your awareness into the present moment. An effective tool for changing your level of stress in the right now.

Most mindfulness practices are designed to help you bring your awareness into the body and into the right now, making it a beautiful tool to help you stop incessantly reviewing the past and rehearsing the future. Where this can get confusing is when people use the word *meditation* when they're actually referring to some type of mindfulness exercise in which you're focusing your mind in a specific direction. Counting your breaths, visualizing, imagining a waterfall, listening to guided audio—all these would be versions of mindfulness. Most of the popular "meditation" apps or guided YouTube videos are shades of mindfulness. They are lovely, and can be incredibly useful for changing your mental state in the right now, but I use mindfulness as a runway *into* meditation. It gives my high-performing students something to do with their busy minds as they are preparing their bodies for the deep rest and surrender that is meditation. I think of mindfulness as the appetizer to the main course of the Ziva Technique—meditation. Mindfulness is a great tool to use if you're stressed in the right now and want to feel better immediately. Similarly, if you have a headache and you take an aspirin, you start feeling results right away. If you're stressed and you listen to a guided mindfulness exercise on your phone, it will help you feel better in the right now.

Meditation, as I define it, is helping you get rid of your stress from the *past*. Your body is a perfect accountant: Every all-nighter you've pulled, every bite of fast food you've ever eaten, and every shot of tequila you've done—it's all stored in your cellular memory. Meditation gives the body deep, healing rest—rest that is actually deeper than sleep. When you give your body the rest it needs, it knows how to heal itself. One of the things it heals itself from is stress. The less stress you have in your body, the easier it is for you to perform at the top of your game.

The specific style of meditation I teach at Ziva has its roots in something called *nishkam karma yoga*, a Sanskrit term meaning "union attained by action hardly taken." It is a six-thousand-year-old practice that is born out of the Vedas, an ancient body of knowledge originating in the Himalayas. The Vedas are the same beautiful body of knowledge from which stem yoga, Ayurvedic medicine, feng shui, and acupuncture. The word *Veda* means knowledge and this knowledge is 1,500 years older than the Great Pyramid of Giza; in other words, this isn't some new age hogwash or hipster-inspired fad.

Nishkam karma meditation requires no effort, no focused concentration, and, thankfully, no struggling to "clear the mind." I like to think of it as the "lazy man's meditation." Instead of trying to force yourself into a cosmic abyss of black-hole nothingness, you allow the body to innocently and spontaneously access a deeply restful state. There is a tool that helps with this; it's called a mantra.

Now, the word *mantra* needs some clarification as well because the wellness industry has hijacked this term. A mantra is not a slogan. It is not an affirmation, such as "I'm a strong, powerful woman!" or "I deserve abundance!" In actuality, the word *mantra*—Sanskrit for "mind vehicle"—is a word or sound used as an anchor to de-excite the nervous system, access more subtle states of consciousness, and induce deep, healing rest.

THE VEDAS: An ancient body of knowledge originating in Northern India, designed to help practitioners find renewal, balance, and wholeness of body, mind, and spirit. They are a human interpretation of the laws of Nature, not a doctrine or dogma.

MANTRA: Sanskrit, from *man* = "mind" and *tra* = "vehicle." A mantra is used as an anchor to de-excite the nervous system, access more subtle states of consciousness, and induce deep, healing rest.

When I teach people face-to-face, students are given their own personalized mantra, which helps them access a verifiable fourth state of consciousness that is different from waking, sleeping, or dreaming. In that fourth state of consciousness, you're giving your body rest that is two to five times deeper than sleep. There will be more on the science behind this concept in chapter 4. One of the main things that differentiates our in-person training from zivaONLINE and the Z Technique are the mantras—what types we use for which training and how long you spend in the meditation portion. In zivaLIVE, which is face-to-face, you're given a personalized but meaningless primordial sound; in zivaONLINE, you are taught a protocol for how to choose your own mantra from a curated list; for the Z Technique and the purposes of learning through a book, we will be using a gentler, universal mantra to access this rest. This deep rest allows you to feel more awake afterward. Imagine a supercharged power nap without the sleep hangover. And instead of needing an hour and a half with your eyes closed, you need only fifteen minutes—bonus: you can do it in your chair at work, on the train, or even with your kids screaming in the next room. The function that helps get rid of the old stresses we have been storing in our cellular and genetic memory is a de-excitation of the nervous system. When you de-excite something, you create order. When you create order in your cells, the stress can start to come up and out in a way that allows your brain to use more of its computing power for the task at hand, instead of wasting that energy managing old stress. This is one of the reasons that meditators tend to get more done in less time.

The specific technique we will be following in *Stress Less, Accomplish More* fuses ancient practices with modern neuroscience. There are elements of the 3 M's distilled specifically for people who are out in the world, who are going after their dreams, and whose lives are a far cry from an insular, monastic existence. What you are about to learn is for people with busy minds and busy lives. ***Mindfulness helps you deal with stress in the present; meditation gets rid of stress from the past; and manifesting helps you clarify your dreams for the future.***

Mindfulness, in its current form, is a derivative of styles of meditation that were originally designed for monks. If you think you might be a monk, this is *not* the book for you. (But I'm guessing the likelihood of you wanting to be a monk is low.) Monastic types are contributing to society in a different way than the rest of the population; their whole life is a meditation. This was news to me when I first started learning. I assumed that monks must be meditating at such an advanced level that they would be vibrating or levitating, but the reality is that if you're in a state of meditation all day, you can afford to do a gentler practice. The rest of us, known in India as "householders"— that is, people with jobs and kids, companies to run, and bills to pay— have less time to meditate. We need a technique designed for us, one that allows us to drop in and access that deep, healing rest regardless of our external settings. That's where the mantra comes into play. You will learn a universal mantra as part of the Z Technique; think of it as an anchor to help you access your least-excited state of awareness, the key to tapping the source of unlimited fulfillment that is inside us all.

The Z Technique is intended for those of us who are householders—who are getting things done and making big things happen on the physical plane. That doesn't mean we can't interact with another plane; it just means we don't spend the majority of our time hanging out there. This style allows us to reap maximum benefits with minimal effort or time. It is designed for high performers. I define a high performer as anyone who wants to be better every day—someone who wants to use their gifts to leave the world better than they found it. Yes, some of us work in high-pressure, "high-stress" environments, but all of us want to get in, get out, and get on with life while life gets better.

HIGH PERFORMER: Someone who wants to be better every day, with the intention to leave the world better than they found it.

Finally, let's dive into the third of the 3 M's: manifesting. Manifesting is simply getting clear about precisely what you want to create in your life, or consciously curating a life you love. It is shocking to me how many people never take the time to get clear on their goals. When I ask my students what their dream job looks like, I often hear them justify their *current* job. When I ask people what their perfect relationship looks like, I often hear vague platitudes about respect and laughter. But just like placing an order at a restaurant, we have to be specific when calling in our dreams.

Most people don't take the time to let Nature know exactly what it is they'd like to create. Manifestation tools help you get crystal clear on your desires so you start to act as if they are on the way. Think of it as placing your order with the great cosmic waitress at the great cosmic restaurant.

MANIFESTING: Designing a life you love. The act of being grateful for what you have while simultaneously imagining your dreams as if they are happening now. The process of manifesting is multifold: 1. Give thanks for what you have. 2. Clarify your goals. 3. Take time to imagine one goal as if it is happening now. 4. Detach from any outcome.

This process has the effect of closing the gap between your desires and those desires becoming reality.

Let me emphasize at the outset that manifesting is *not* "magical thinking." This isn't something you simply wish into being; you still have to get off the couch and take inspired action. Manifesting is the acknowledgment that thoughts become things. Once you learn the Z Technique, you'll have a daily practice of manifesting directly after the deep rest and connection that meditation provides, which is a powerful time to create.

What makes manifesting so effective directly after meditation is that the meditation is helping you access that verifiable fourth state of consciousness, which is different from waking, sleeping, or dreaming. In this fourth state of consciousness, your right brain and left brain are functioning in unison. This is very similar to the state you are in when you fall into and out of sleep. Every time the brain transitions between waking and sleeping, it moves through a short window of this fourth state of consciousness, which is something I call "the bliss field." We will also access this during the meditation portion of the Z Technique.

It has long been known that visualizing your ideal life as you fall asleep is a great way to fast-track your dreams to fruition. Neville Goddard wrote about this back in 1944 in his book *Feeling Is the Secret*. The amazing gift you'll be giving yourself with your twice-a-day practice is triple the opportunities to plant these seeds for your future.

Just as you can achieve a deeper stretch and greater flexibility at the end of a workout, when your muscles are already warmed up and malleable, so, too, is manifestation a more effective tool at the end of meditation. In my personal experience and in guiding thousands of high achievers through this process, I have found that practicing meditation and manifesting together is so much more powerful than doing either on its own. You could meditate all day long, but if you never take the time to get clear about what it is you want, it's much harder for Nature to bring you your order. Similarly, you could make hundreds of vision boards and hang them all around your home, or practice *The Secret* day in and day out, but if your body and mind are riddled with stress, you may not believe you deserve to step into your dream. The trick here is that we don't get what we want in life, we get what we believe we deserve.

There are some schools of thought that suggest your desires are divinely inspired—that manifestation actually precedes the desire. This idea holds that your impulse for something is actually Nature letting you know what is already making its way toward you. You know how you can feel the wind rushing toward you through the subway tunnel before you ever hear the train approaching or actually see its lights? Or how you see the pink and orange clouds before the sun actually rises above the horizon at dawn? Desire and manifestation can be thought of as operating in the same way. (This is rather advanced, and we will revisit this concept once you have more practice under your belt.)

» The Meditation Shame Spiral

It doesn't matter what type of meditation you're practicing. If you don't have any training, it's very possible you'll be judging yourself based on misinformation. Meditation is deceptively simple, but *don't confuse simplicity for weakness*. As lovely as it would be to be able to give the mind a command to shut up, or turn off our built-in hearing aids, this is not the point. There's nowhere on planet Earth that is completely silent, not even the caves of the Himalayas. If you sit down to meditate and a dog barks in the distance, a siren screams by, or your right bum cheek falls asleep—and your mind registers those sounds or sensations, as well as all the thoughts and images that go along with them—suddenly you're on a mental field trip. (So much for achieving oneness with the universe.) Surely monks would never deign to let their minds wander to such unprofound things as their neighbor's cranky pug or a tingling butt.

As a result, you chalk that meditation session up as a failure, and further, you see yourself as someone who has failed. The next time you sit down to meditate, you're determined to do better, thinking, *I'm* not *going to think this time. I'm* not *going to think this time. I'm* not *going to think this time* . . . which is, of course, thinking. So you finish another meditation, and not only did you "fail" to clear your mind again, you have the added guilt of a second failed meditation attempt. You grit your teeth and buckle down for a third attempt, this time in a super-squishy seat in a perfectly soundproof room, so there are no possible distractions to stop you from reaching nirvana. Everything is going great; you're comfortable, you're relaxed, you run absolutely no risk of being disrupted by a noise from outside . . . and then your stomach rumbles. No problem—you manage to pull yourself back in, relishing the silence of your surroundings. Really, really relishing it. *I mean, this has got to be the quietest place I've ever been. I can't even hear the ambient noise of water in the pipes. Way to go, self, for paying a little extra for the deluxe soundproofing package! The guy at the hardware store said it would be worth it, and he was totally right and . . .* crap. Now you're thinking about how great you are at meditating and your home-improvement projects, no longer in the moment of thought-free Neverland. And you've "failed" at meditation yet again.

Rack up enough so-called failures in a row, and you'll grow discouraged and eventually give up, because who wants to feel like they're failing at something on a daily basis? You mess up, so you try harder, but the very effort that helps you succeed in most other areas of your life just guarantees another failure at meditation.

The Meditation Shame Spiral, I have found, is especially prevalent among high achievers. They're often reluctant to even attempt meditation because they fear they won't be any good at it. "I am afraid to even try, because my mind is just too busy to meditate," they insist. "My mind is too busy to achieve anything like bliss."

Meditation often feels intimidating for high achievers, who are used to doing and succeeding; they're used to picking up new skills easily and have often built their identities on their ability to stare down every challenge. But here's the secret they don't like to talk about when they dust off their trophy cases: They naturally gravitate toward the very things that highlight their strengths and avoid the things that don't. In other words, they like to operate in the areas where they know they can succeed. While this feels nice and validates the ego, it doesn't lead to a life of growth.

Did I see you cringe a little as you read that last comment? Did it strike a little too close to home? Here's the thing: I understand you, achievers, because *I am one of you.* I am the most achievement-driven achiever who ever tried to achieve at achieving, so I know what I'm talking about when I say our biggest fear as success-driven individuals is failure. And we usually aren't particularly good at it, for the simple reason that we haven't had much experience with it. So when we're faced with a new skill set that seems like it may not play to our strengths, our first reaction is usually to dismiss it and move on to something where success is much more likely.

If this sounds familiar, I would encourage you to go into this book with an open mind. The techniques you'll learn here are very different from the oh-so-frustrating "clear your mind" directives you probably received in the past. Take another look at the practice of meditation specifically because it's just that—a *practiced* discipline. Even the most experienced in the field are constantly growing, hungry to discover new facets of their potential, to up-level their brains to higher states of consciousness, and to access a deeper connectedness. In other words, we are all constantly in a state of improvement. You already possess the ability to be a successful meditator because you have the ability to think a thought. More on that soon, but as I said earlier, ***we meditate to get good at life, not to get good at meditation***. No one cares if we are good at meditation, though I wish they did—I love being the best at things (and I suspect you do, too). But the ultimate goal is never to become a world-class meditator. That's just silly. What would be the point? Meditation is not a party trick you do to show off to your friends; meditation is the means to an end. The goal is, ultimately, the innumerable benefits of meditation and how they can shape our lives, enhance our performance, and improve our interactions in the world.

It is impossible to lose at meditation. Let me say that again: *It is impossible to lose at meditation.* Every act of delving into your least-excited state, every inspired decision you make as a result of your practice, every moment that you realize that you are enough is a victory. In other words, every time you engage in the practice, you're winning. Achievers afraid to try meditation because they fear they won't be good at it should let that sink in: Practicing the Z Technique guarantees you at least two successes a day.

» So Why Meditate?

So why does any of this matter? Even if the practice truly is quick and simple, what do we really gain or lose by incorporating it as a nonnegotiable part of our daily routine?

In the upcoming chapters, we will take a closer look at stress—its origins and its impact on every aspect of our health, down to the cellular level in our bodies. We will also examine the neuroscience behind meditation and the way it positively impacts the human brain in both objective and subjective measures. For now, though, I would simply like you to consider the very practical, utilitarian side of the question: Why should you dedicate any of your very precious and limited minutes, every day, to meditation?

Simply put, because it creates more time. *Would you be willing to invest 2 percent of your day if you knew it would improve the other 98 percent?* If so, buckle up, because that's exactly what this book will teach you to do.

Let's dive deeper into the concept of time, because that seems to be the most universal concern of all would-be meditators—especially high-performing, outcome-driven personalities. I hear it constantly: They are reluctant to try meditation because "I'm too busy to meditate" or "I barely have time to go to the bathroom or eat lunch, much less spend a quarter of an hour just sitting."

Guess what? They're right. I don't have time for that, either. That's the reason Ziva is so perfectly suited for people who are doers: It *is* doing. Just because the mind thinks involuntarily during meditation doesn't mean it isn't working; this tool goes after the root cause of stress, the thing that triggers so many negative physical and emotional responses.

Think about it: When your phone is plugged in, it's not "just sitting," is it? Of course not. It's charging so it'll be ready to be the most effective tool it can be when you need to use it. When your computer does that forced-shutdown thing, where it spends fifteen minutes upgrading while that little spinning wheel mocks you, is it "just sitting"? Sure, it may feel like that—it might even look like it—but your computer is actually engaged in a series of system cleanups that have been programmed specifically for the sake of making it a more efficient, more effective, and more powerful machine than it was before.

What if you never took the time to charge your phone? What if you never rebooted your computer so it could install updates? Would your tools be operating at optimum efficiency? When you don't allow your mind the chance to refresh and rejuvenate itself, you're denying it the chance to reach peak performance, and possibly even running it down to zero, at which point it's physically incapable of performing the very tasks it was designed to do.

I've got plenty more of these analogies, but I'm going to stop here because I'm pretty sure you get the idea. The point is, when you engage in meditation that is made for *you*—not for monks—you're *literally creating time*. You are optimizing your cognitive performance capabilities so you can get more done in less time. The Z Technique is the very opposite of doing nothing; it's consciously and methodically creating an optimized space from which to operate with superior equipment and with your maximized abilities. Viewed in this way, meditation is so much more than "just sitting"; it's updating and defragging your mental hardware so you can more effectively run whatever software you have as the operating system of your life, be it Christianity, Judaism, Islam, Hinduism, Buddhism, Baha'i, any number of self-help regimens, secular humanism—pretty much everything but nihilism. (Though I have no doubt meditation would prove beneficial for nihilists, too.) ***Meditation is not a belief system or*** *religious practice; it is a technique that will allow you to remove stress from your body while strengthening your mind.*

I can tell you all about the scientifically verifiable benefits, as well as the anecdotal ones confirmed by my fifteen-thousand-plus students. I can cite scores of recent articles quoting high achievers who credit meditation as a key aspect of their success. I can even point to dozens of Fortune 500 companies that have embraced the practice company-wide. I can also tell you why various industry leaders, innovators, and influencers meditate. The one thing I cannot do is tell you why *you* should incorporate meditation into your daily routine. That ultimately has to come from you. You have to be the one to identify not only the goal but why you are pursuing it—the motivation that reaches beyond the moment the goal is reached. In other words, it's great to celebrate crossing the finish line, but what prompted you to run the race in the first place?

Here's some good news: *You don't have to have your life figured out to begin a meditation practice.* Seriously. Just about every other self-help or personal improvement plan hinges on figuring out profound truths about yourself, your driving forces, and your inspirations *before* you begin to experience the positive results. Meditation is a tool that can actually help you discover those things along the way. As you begin to practice the plan laid out in this book, you'll find that rather than being the goal itself, the Z Technique is actually just a means of moving your mind, intuition, creativity, and even your physical body toward realizing your goals and clarifying your motivations. As we discussed above, the word *mantra* literally means "mind vehicle," moving you from one place to another. The only thing that matters, at this point, is the intention and desire to improve your current state of being. If you have that, you can begin on the journey and let the rest sort itself out as you go.

Are you ready for your first homework assignment? Write down your intention for picking up this book, no matter how vague, silly, or ambiguous it may feel right now. You could write something general, like "I want to enjoy my life more." Or you could be much more specific, like "I want to get a promotion within the next six months." You could even be more subjective, such as "I want my family to find common ground about politics" or "I want to be a better parent" or "I want to be a stronger force for good in the world." Even if you have to say "I don't know why I feel compelled to try meditation, but I'm out of other ideas," that's fine, too. There is absolutely no judgment here. (Remember, I got into meditating in part for the noble goal of not wanting gray hair in my twenties.)

I am reading *Stress Less, Accomplish More* because . . .

_____

_____

_____

This is how stress is affecting my performance today:

_____

_____

_____

_____

On a scale of 1–10 (1 being the worst, 10 being the best), this is how I rate my:

Sleep:
Work Performance:
Relationships:
Stress:
Intuition:
Creativity:
Health:

Don't skip this assignment. It can be tough to take an honest look at your relationship with stress. But seriously, don't skip it. This will help you to gauge your success as you start a daily practice. It will also be fun to revisit this once you finish the book and have some meditation under your belt.

Once you have these answers written down, I would like you to give some thought to one more thing: your excuse for not trying meditation sooner.

Maybe you're just learning about it for the first time. Maybe you had some misconceptions about what it was really all about. Maybe you used to practice but fell out of the habit. I suspect that at least some of you haven't tried it because it sounded like a bunch of hippy-dippy, woo-woo magic talk. And I'm sure that for the vast majority of readers, simply not having the time for yet another thing on your calendar is at least a contributing factor in avoiding meditation. Whatever your reason, make a mental note of it—and be honest. The important thing is to be frank and authentic. Meditation is about accessing the best possible version of you, so don't be afraid to be transparent as we begin this journey.

» With That in Mind . . .

As we move forward in this book, I would encourage you to be gentle with yourself. Don't think you have to set out to be the best meditator in all the land. Don't worry if you find your mind far busier than you would like it to be. Don't sweat the Sanskrit words and scientific terms I'll be throwing at you.

Most important, let go of your preconceived notions of what meditation "should" look like and instead give yourself permission to enter this with beginner's mind. Enjoy this as a wholly new (but time-tested) method for relieving stress and preparing your mind and body for heightened awareness and engagement with life.

This may all still sound a little nebulous, but I promise that it will begin to get clearer and more tangible as we progress. Right now, I just want you to ask yourself if you're ready to *commit to the intention* of meditating. That's it; there's nothing more required of you at this point. Just commit to the intention—that's enough for us to get started, and it may be enough to change the trajectory of the rest of your life.

Ziva Case Study 1

From $70,000 of Debt to $1.2 Million Earned in One Year

MARI CARMEN, ENTREPRENEUR

I saw Emily for the first time at a business mastermind group where she was speaking. There was something attractive about her, beyond her appearance and contagious smile. She was tapped into something more profound; her glow came from within. She was powerful yet calm and confident, and I knew right away I wanted some of what she was having.

Two months after seeing her onstage, I rearranged my schedule and traveled to New York City to attend her zivaLIVE course. I was already a meditator (of sorts), but I knew without a doubt that there was more to it, and I trusted that she could show me the way.

My situation was not terrible; life was not "that bad." I had retired from a successful corporate job, I was happily married, the kids were almost out of the house, and I had started my own business in 2014. I was on the way to continued success . . . or so I thought.

Okay, the truth that no one knows is that I had accumulated $70,000 in debt and somehow burned through my $200,000 in savings in two short years. My new business was in the red, big time. My confidence was dwindling quickly; I was scattered and felt needy, which I hated. Despite all these demands, I knew the answers must reside within me, and that somewhere in this whole mess, there had to be a lesson I needed to learn.

However, I had absolutely no idea *how to access* those answers that supposedly resided within me.

Right after Emily's first class, I felt better. Maybe it was a psychological high, but who cares! When first starting meditation, I'm not sure if it matters if it's a placebo effect. I knew I was doing the right thing for me. So I made a commitment to my twice-per-day meditations.

I didn't have any "extra" time in the morning for meditation, so I moved the alarm clock back. In the beginning it was just fifteen minutes, but now I wake up thirty minutes earlier than before. I use the first fifteen minutes for my meditation and the rest to joyfully take my time getting ready for the day. It is such a powerful psychological shift to feel ahead of schedule and prepared for the day, versus rushed and late right out of the gate.

After the first two weeks, I kept "forgetting" the second meditation. All the while, my sleep improved, I had more time, and my skin started to look better and more rested. Even though I was spending less time sleeping, I was more energized, and I began to be able to hear those answers that I knew resided inside me.

So, I thought, *If once-a-day meditation can do this much good, what could committing to twice daily do?* I decided to cut the BS and start "remembering" the afternoon meditation. I have to admit, at times it felt like torture. I feel there is still a part of me that wants to "forget about it," but I can't, and here's why.

After one year of consistently taking two Ziva meditation breaks per day, I have:

> Added three more hours of productivity to my day. Here's the thing: The clarity that meditation gives me allows me to make decisions faster, see answers to challenging situations more quickly, and come up with new content (for blogs, a course, a third book) much more easily. I feel my brain capacity expanding.

> My energy levels have always been reasonable, but now I have double the energy I used to have. I'm well into my fifties and more vibrant than ever!

> With more time in the day and more energy, my work performance has skyrocketed. My mind is not

cluttered anymore as I go through my workday, so the things I'm building are of higher quality, and my creativity is solid. I have exceeded my own performance expectations.

> I landed a TED Talk, which was one of the most "stressful" opportunities I have ever faced. You can't re-record it, it's live, you only get one shot to do it right . . . and I nailed it!

> I finally found the answers I needed (turns out, they were inside me all along) to revamp my business and move in a different direction. This resulted in an increase in sales from $80,000 to $1,200,000 in one year. I am consistently attracting the kind of client who is ready for this lady boss to empower them to reach new heights.

What else can I say? Meditation is not about changing who you are, moving to a cave, or sitting cross-legged in a dark room waiting for something to happen. I have worked my buns off, and it hasn't all been easy, but it's been so incredibly rewarding.

I can't imagine quitting now. There's no going back for me, because the results are clear. Ziva has transformed my life.

TAPPING THE SOURCE

TAKE A DEEP BREATH, LET YOUR SHOULDERS DROP, AND GET
this: All that rushing around, multitasking, and double-booking is
making you less efficient. We have come to equate being busy with
being productive. We have glorified being busy. We feel like downtime is wasted time. We're wrong.

» Stress ≠ Productivity

Like so many people, I used to feel that stress equaled productivity—
that it was a necessary part of success. That was pre-meditation. The
contrast with post-meditation couldn't be starker. Now I see all that
stress and worry as wasted energy. After a decade of meditating regularly, I was invited to give a keynote presentation at A-Fest, a bio-
hacking conference in Greece. There were some heavy hitters in the
room, and the presentation was being filmed and distributed to over
2 million people. It was my first keynote and my first time using slides;
I had a feeling this talk could change the trajectory of my career, yet I
felt so calm before I went onstage. Sure, there was a heightened sense
of being alive, but before I had a daily practice, you could pretty much
watch me vibrate before speaking publicly. Now I allow myself to be

a vessel for knowledge to flow through and serve the audience. The worry and stress are replaced with confidence that Nature has my back.

My talk in Greece was a career highlight. I spoke in front of a full house, and my presentation ended with a standing ovation. People can tell if you're there to serve them or to serve yourself. Stress keeps you in survival mode, which keeps you focused on yourself. Meditation helps you get out of that primal "fight or flight" mode, so you can give more generously and access creative ideas, even in high-stress situations.

What did it take for me to gain that confidence, to thoroughly prepare ahead of time, and to go out and nail the challenge? Setting aside time each day for mindfulness, meditation, and manifesting.

Yes, I'm talking about giving up some of your most valuable resource every day. We all kill plenty of time during the day doing other things—watching TV, checking social media, watching cat videos on YouTube—that don't improve our productivity, so what's another few minutes that *will* actually help you increase your performance capabilities and enable you to become a better, more efficient human?

Some of the busiest people you can think of make time for meditation every day. It's not because they have copious amounts of free time. It's because they have done the research on their own brains and bodies, and they now know the opportunity cost of *not* meditating. At Ziva, we love working with high performers, people who are lit up about their mission. Stacy London, from TLC's *What Not to Wear*, is one of them. She uses fashion as a way to help people feel more comfortable in their skin regardless of their size, shape, or age. When she came to Ziva to learn meditation, she wasn't convinced it could help her. "I was one of those people who always thought I didn't have time to meditate," she admitted. "Who has that kind of time, right? Now I realize that was such an excuse. The busier you are, the more beneficial this kind of meditation is."

What most people haven't experienced yet is that your mind and your body already have the capacity to meet—and exceed—all the demands you put on them. But stress straps us with emotional blinders that block, and ultimately deplete, our power to tap into those reserves of energy and ability. When we allow our brains to recharge and defrag, we are actually building our mental capacity and increasing our creativity. If you think of your job, chores, and demands as the race you're running in life, then meditation is your training—the mental fitness plan that allows you to achieve at a high level in every aspect of your life.

Meditation helps you accomplish your tasks much more quickly and more elegantly. Think about that for a moment: For the thirty minutes you spend in meditation each day (total), you're becoming a much more effective person. You'll meet challenges and solve problems in much less time than they would normally take. When Michael Trainer, the national director of the Global Poverty Project and former executive producer of the Global Citizen Festival, came to me to learn meditation, he was surprised at what he gained. "A greater sense of equanimity, relaxation, clarity," he reported. "I think it's unequivocally one of the best investments you could make."

Here's the ROI on your thirty minutes a day of meditation: You'll get more done, be more relaxed, and achieve goals you never believed attainable. You'll increase your problem-solving powers, be more open to creative solutions, and have more energy to deal with adversity. Your capacity for handling setbacks will expand, and you'll marvel at your ability to get things done.

» Getting Meditation "Right"

As you'll recall from chapter 1, the meditation portion of the Ziva Technique is called *nishkam karma yoga*, which is just a fancy way of saying "union attained by action hardly taken"—in other words, meditation for the busy person.

In this type of meditation, you're basically giving your body and brain deep rest—rest that is up to *five times* deeper than sleep!—so it can release a lifetime of accumulated stress. People's familiarity with other styles of meditation often leads them to think there's a "good" or "perfect" way to meditate, which often creates frustration in us less-than-perfect human beings.

The reason I created the Ziva Technique—and one of the reasons it's becoming more popular—is that you can do it anywhere, anytime, as long as you have a few minutes. You don't need robes or incense; you don't have to wait for quiet, or until you're calm and everything is sunshine and roses. All you need is your mantra, some training, and a place to sit. We will keep revisiting this concept, so don't worry about having to "clear your mind"—that's a misconception about meditation. So, if you've ever tried meditation and felt like a failure because you couldn't quiet your mind, don't panic. As we discussed in chapter 1, the mind thinks involuntarily just like the heart beats involuntarily. This practice is mercifully simple, but the payoff is incredible.

» Your Brain and Body on Meditation

People come to meditation for a multitude of reasons. Sometimes they're dealing with anxiety, depression, migraines, or insomnia. Sometimes they've been diagnosed with an incurable illness. More and more, I'm seeing people come to meditation as a performance-enhancing tool. In fact, I like to think of Ziva as *the* meditation for improved performance—and it's exactly this practice that I've adapted for this book.

Over the past forty years, neurological researchers have been proving what meditators have known for six thousand years. Science has found that meditation increases the gray and white matter in your brain. More specifically, it enlarges the structure that connects the right and left sides of your brain, known as the corpus callosum. That's valuable because we tend to be very left brain–focused in our day-to-day lives. The left brain is in charge of critical, analytical thought—everything from language to balancing the checkbook and keeping track of responsibilities. But the right brain is the creative side. It's where intuition, artistic ability, and creative problem-solving reside.

Meditation improves the connection between your analytical side and your intuitive side (that is, your critical mind and your creative mind), allowing your brain to start working in true harmony. When you meditate, your insula (the brain's empathy center) improves communication with your dorsomedial prefrontal cortex (the part of the brain where you process information about unfamiliar people). As any relationship expert, therapist, or well-meaning but slightly pushy parent will tell you, communication is the key to a healthy relationship. When you enable two distinct but vital parts of your brain to connect, engage, and transmit information back and forth, you're building essential communication between different aspects of your psyche. And I don't mean wait-three-days-to-respond-to-a-text-and-then-send-an-ambiguous-emoji communication. I'm talking the kind of communication that happens when you sit down with your partner and look into each other's eyes, baring your souls and speaking without reservation, fear, or pretense. I mean the kind of open and honest communication that tends to happen over a second bottle of wine or a third pint of Ben & Jerry's (or both—no judgment). *When the disparate parts of your brain are communicating at such an intense level, neuropathways become neuro-superhighways as you build, connect, and reinforce those connections.*

These connections between your creativity and your analysis are the source of the all-important "sixth sense": intuition. Intuition can help guide you to better, more creative solutions to your daily challenges; it can also heighten your awareness by making your mind more effective at both taking in and evaluating situations before you're even conscious that you've given the matter any thought. You tap into a whole new level of efficiency because your creativity helps you problem-solve at work and in relationships.

For example, University of Arizona researchers had human resources managers try mindfulness for eight weeks and then analyzed their decision-making skills, their focus under pressure, and their overall stress levels. Compared to managers who didn't take the class, the mindfulness practitioners had much better focus and could stay on task much longer. Best of all, they reported feeling less stressed in general.

Relieving you of stress and anxiety—which can undermine your focus and diminish your problem-solving capabilities—is what this book is all about. In one of the purest tests of what meditation does for the mind, Carnegie Mellon researchers asked thirty-five unemployed men and women to try meditation or, for comparison, relaxation exercises. These people, as you can imagine, were under tremendous stress as they desperately scrambled to find jobs. After just three days, the meditation group felt immensely better. Even more remarkably, brain scans found better communication between the areas of the brain that process stress and those related to focus and calm. When the researchers checked back in after four months, the meditation group had much lower levels of stress-related hormones in their blood. They felt more optimistic about their job search and more productive in meeting their day-to-day challenges and goals.[1]

These volunteers also had less overall inflammation, one of the great dangers of our modern diet and lifestyle. When you pull a muscle or bump into a doorframe, your body's response is to rush biological healing mechanisms to the injured area. Blood flow to the injury increases as your immune system delivers the proteins and chemicals that will repair the damage. It's a great system—unless it's overtaxed. So many things in and around us provoke this inflammatory response: poor diet, stress, and toxins in our environment, to name just a few. For some people, this constant exposure can lead to runaway inflammation, triggering autoimmune disorders like allergies, diabetes, lupus, and Crohn's disease. But you can tame the inflammation in your body through meditation. By reducing the acidic (and therefore inflammatory) effects of stress and improving sleep, your body is better able to heal itself and tamp down inflammation. The result is that you feel better, breathe easier, and manage weight and health with ease.

Lindsey Clayton, a celebrity trainer, was taking a big professional step forward when her health began to fall apart. "I was transitioning from musical theatre to fitness, and I suddenly found myself in a very high-demand job," she explained. Lindsey loved the new career, which included starring in a TV show on Bravo, but she was putting in eighty hours a week with no days off: "I was becoming very successful very quickly, but I had stopped caring for myself. Staring in the mirror on New Year's Eve, I could see the toll—it was written all over my face." Her anxiety had reached an all-time high. She felt overworked, unmotivated, frustrated, and depressed. "My skin looked dry, my hair dull, and my eyes sad, and my knee was still swollen and painful from a four-month-old injury." After almost a year of resisting a friend's suggestion that she try meditation, Lindsey finally gave in: "I built up the courage to attend an intro talk at Ziva Meditation."

After just a few sessions, she began to notice a difference—a difference that led to a life-changing experience. Her knee injury healed, her frustration dissipated, and she started working smarter instead of longer. Lindsey was able to cut back on her crazy hours while also getting even more work done. After learning to meditate, she noticed a dramatic improvement in her physical and emotional health: "I feel so much happier, and I can look in the mirror and see how much healthier my skin and hair are. Most important, I have the energy to create the life I truly want to live."

When you're healthy and your body is calm, you're able to use your energy for your real work on this planet. Your life may continue to be "busy," but it won't be chaotic. You'll find you can manage the problems and challenges far more elegantly, without the drama.

» Stress Less, Accomplish More

Why does meditation have such a pronounced effect on your work and personal performance? In a nutshell, it rewires your brain to be more efficient. The technical term is *neuroplasticity,* which is a fancy word for the brain's ability to change itself. The brain can become more innovative and creative when it comes to problem solving. It can even appear in tests to have grown *younger* after years of practice. How does it do what scientists previously thought was impossible? Meditation relieves stress from the body by de-exciting the nervous system, which allows the brain to operate in its most effective way possible, rather than from perpetual crisis mode.

If stress is so bad for us as humans, then why does it exist in the first place? In order to understand this, we need to step back in time ten thousand years or so, to the days when humankind was still hunting and gathering for survival. There you are, minding your own business, picking berries and thinking about what you want to paint on the walls of your cave that evening. Suddenly, a saber-toothed tiger leaps out of the woods with the intent to kill. Your body automatically launches into a series of chemical reactions known as the fight-or-flight stress response.

First, your digestive tract floods with acid to shut down digestion, because it takes a lot of energy to digest your food, and you need all hands on deck to fight or flee. That same acid will then seep into your skin so that you won't taste very good if that tiger bites into you. Your blood will start to thicken and coagulate so if you do get bitten into, you won't necessarily bleed to death. Your vision will go from wide-scope to tunnel vision, so you're not distracted from your opponent. Your bladder and bowels will evacuate so you're lighter on your feet and able to move quickly. (Those nervous poos you get before a major presentation? That's your body having a primal reaction and trying to protect you.) Your heart rate, cortisol, and adrenaline levels will increase. Your immune system goes to the back burner, because who cares if you're going to get cancer if you're about to be killed by a tiger? Again, you need all hands on deck to fight or flee this predatory attack.

This series of chemical reactions has been custom-designed over millions of years to keep your meat-suit alive, and it's very, very useful if your most pressing demand is to avoid becoming lunch for Stone Age carnivores. But in the modern world, when you undergo that process several times a day, every day, it fries your nervous system, overtaxes your immune system, and leaves you susceptible to viruses and bacteria. What we fail to realize is that there's a massive reservoir of calm and natural intelligence within us—including our body's ability to heal and maintain itself—waiting for us to tap. When you properly manage stress, your body simply works better. It is this constant, low-grade, chronic stress that is making us stupid, sick, and slow as a species. Thankfully, this doesn't have to be the norm.

This fight-or-flight stress reaction has become largely maladaptive for our modern-day demands. The good news here is that as we learn to meditate and make it a nonnegotiable part of our daily routine, we can not only get out of fight or flight but also start to tap into the massive reservoir of energy and natural intelligence that resides within us. When you properly manage stress (instead of letting stress manage you), your body and brain can take all that energy previously wasted on imaginary tiger attacks and start to channel it into all the things you want to create in your lifetime.

Once your brain reaches the right/left brain synchronicity that meditation offers, the world opens up to you. Solutions to everyday problems are much easier to find. I've heard it from students over and over again, and I've experienced it in my own life. It might be quickly solving a disagreement between your kids or your coworkers; it might be figuring out how to get through a demanding workday; it might be as simple as finding a rock-star parking space.

Major corporations are starting to realize what meditation can do for company performance, and they're beginning to offer it to their employees. Aetna, one of the largest insurance companies in the world, offered mindfulness courses to its workforce, and more than a quarter of its fifty thousand employees signed up, reported the *New York Times*. On average, the people who took the course experienced a 28 percent reduction in stress levels, a 20 percent improvement in sleep quality, and a 19 percent reduction in pain. Crucially, the Aetna practitioners also became much more effective at their jobs, gaining, on average, 62 minutes a week of productivity and saving the company $3,000 per employee every year. Demand for the programs continues to rise; at Aetna, every class is overbooked.[2] And all this came from them practicing only one of the 3 M's you're going to learn about in this book!

» Adaptation Energy

What creates this newfound ability to accomplish more? Meditation helps you access an internal resource I call *adaptation energy*. Adaptation energy is your ability to handle a demand or a change of expectation. It's the energy we draw on to manage our ever-growing to-do lists—and most of us are running on empty. Don't believe me? Let's put this into a real-life scenario: Imagine waking up late on Monday morning—your alarm failed to go off. That's a drag, but you can shrug it off. You cut your morning routine short and race out the door on time.

ADAPTATION ENERGY: Your ability to handle a demand or a change of expectation.

But then you get stuck in traffic. Everyone's slowing down to stare at a guy changing his tire on the side of the road. The backup has added fifteen minutes to your commute. *Oof!* You bang the steering wheel and burn up a bit more of your precious adaptation energy.

You park the car and then swing by the coffee shop to grab some java for work—only to find out they're in the middle of brewing a new batch. "Here, have this chamomile tea on the house," says the overly cheery barista. That's the last thing you want, and now you're fuming and left with even less adaptation energy in the tank. The day escalates from there: Your boss yells at you for being late; you miss a meeting that somehow disappeared from your calendar. When you get home, your spouse doesn't understand why you're in such a bad mood. Then you're standing at the sink drinking some water—or perhaps something a little stronger—and the glass slips out of your hand and shatters on the kitchen floor.

Suddenly you're either crying or punching the kitchen wall or both. And it's all over a $2 glass from Crate and Barrel that you can easily replace tomorrow.

So what's causing the involuntary reaction? It's certainly not the stupid broken glass. It's the fact that somewhere around two o'clock that day, you tapped out of adaptation energy. As a result, any future demands leave your body with no choice but to freak out. From that point forward, any problems—no matter how big or small—become overwhelming. Drop that glass on a day when you have sufficient sleep, few demands, and plenty of adaptation energy, and you'll barely wince. You're not *choosing* to flip out over something trivial; it happens because your well of adaptation energy is depleted.

So how do you refill your reservoirs of adaptation energy? Meditation. It's the very thing that allows you to tap into the source of energy. ***If you have effective tools to manage your stress levels and anxiety, even the biggest "setbacks" can become opportunities for growth and innovation.***

» Why Meditation Matters

Yes, many people start meditation to become more productive. Once you start, you'll want to keep doing it for the clarity and energy it gives you. If you're unsure about those rewards or still believe you can't devote time to sitting still, consider the remarkably busy—not to mention successful—people who do make time for meditation: Oprah Winfrey, Ray Dalio, Congressman Tim Ryan, Kobe Bryant, Tim Ferriss, Michelle Williams, Channing Tatum, Ellen DeGeneres, Meghan Markle, and Hugh Jackman, just to name a few. Tim Ferriss, bestselling author of *The 4-Hour Workweek* and host of one of the world's most popular podcasts, in which he interviews high performers, shared that 90 percent of his guests start their day with meditation.

Arianna Huffington reported from the World Economic Forum that the big news at Davos was that all the CEOs are outing themselves as meditators. Oprah Winfrey says that meditation makes her 1,000 times more productive. And the celebrities, entrepreneurs, and change-makers I've trained tell me meditation has increased their intuition, their energy levels, and, ultimately, their success.

Most important, you'll find that meditation allows you to use your desires as an indicator of how best to deliver your gifts to the world. Instead of being under the illusion that your happiness lies on the other side of any person, place, or financial goal, you'll realize that what you seek is already within you. Meditation will become not only a practice to transform your own life, but one you can use to transform the lives of the people and the world around you for the better.

» A Note About the End-of-Chapter Exercises

We all want to perform at the top of our game, but how well we execute when faced with challenges is the single most significant separating factor between high performers and those who get stuck somewhere short of their full potential. We are all brilliant singers in the shower; everyone crushes the presentation in their living room the night before. But it doesn't matter how well you perform until it's go time. Having the tools to get your body and mind prepared to perform can make all the difference. That is what these pull-out exercises at the end of selected chapters are designed to give you. Some are "Eyes-Closed Exercises"—that is, directed-focus mental techniques. Others are "Eyes-Open Exercises"—these are designed to be practical tools for thinking about the topic in a different way.

These exercises are designed to help with real-life situations or to be used as a boost between your regular, twice-daily Z Technique times. Think of them as a quick hit of bliss or a midday reset to help you transform your fear into fuel and your stress into strength so you can actually start to enjoy high-pressure situations instead of running from them! You will learn how to use these supplementary techniques on your own so they become second nature, transforming your default stress response from "fight or flight" to "stay and play." It doesn't matter if you've won an Oscar, are an Olympic athlete, or have started your own business—everyone gets nervous in high-demand situations. Top performers are those people who are able to consistently flip the script on fear. Bravery is not the absence of fear; it is feeling the fear and doing it anyway.

Some of the exercises are simply practical tips to incorporate into your day to reduce stress or improve performance; some use the breath to reset the brain and body; and others use visualization—helping you to see things in your mind that you want to show up in your life. As the late self-help legend Wayne Dyer said, "You'll see it when you believe it."

If you prefer to listen to an audio version and have me guide you through, many of the exercises are available at www.zivameditation.com/bookbonus.

Eyes-Closed Exercise

The 2x Breath

This simple but powerful breathing technique can keep you from spiraling into a cesspool of stress and help you become more present in the current moment.

You can't negotiate with your stress. When you are in fight-or-flight mode, the amygdala takes over. The amygdala is an ancient, preverbal part of the brain. This is why it doesn't work when you simply tell yourself to relax (or worse, when someone *else* tells you to relax). The part of you that is stressed doesn't understand language. Instead, we have to shift the body physically or chemically. That is what the 2x Breath technique will do.

The magic is in doubling the length of the exhale. This calms the vagus nerve, one of the main connections between the brain and the body. As you relax it, information can start to flow from your brain to your body and vice versa, opening you up to solutions from Nature as they present themselves.

1. Start by inhaling through your nose for 2 counts. Then exhale through your mouth for 4 counts. You can even start with your eyes open, walking around the room if you're really amped.
2. Again, inhale through your nose for 2, then exhale through your mouth for 4.
3. Repeat. Inhale for 2, exhale for 4. If you're calmer now,

you can move to a seated position and close your eyes. Continue for about 3 minutes or 15 breaths.

4. Once you're back in your body and in the right now, think of three things you're most grateful for in this moment. No, really. List them. It's impossible to be afraid and grateful at the same time. One emotion makes the other more acute, then evaporates it.

Take note of how you feel before and after this exercise. It is simple on purpose. Many of my students share that taking a few minutes to practice the 2x Breath is enough to keep anxiety attacks at bay if they catch them early enough. Now give yourself a big internal high five and go about your day knowing there is power and integrity in tending to your mental fitness.

» **3** «

STRESS MAKES YOU STUPID

STRESS CAN BE A GOOD THING WHEN IT ENABLES YOUR BODY to survive for another day. But is that really the metric by which you want to be evaluating your life? "Well, I wasn't torn to shreds by wild beasts, so today was a win." In order to lift ourselves out of a perpetual state of fight or flight, we need to take daily action to eradicate the backlog of stresses stored in our cellular memory so that we are able to function in a state far superior to survival mode, which is where most of modern society has become stuck.

There are some modern-day high-demand situations in which the fight-or-flight chemical reactions can be relevant. For instance, if you get jumped in a back alley or need to lift a car off a baby, you'll probably be grateful for hardwired biological responses that enable your body and mind to work in tandem to save your life or someone else's. And there are even forms of exercise and health routines that induce hormesis, or "good stress," in the body. Good stress looks like a cold shower, an ice bath, a sauna, or high-intensity interval training. These are short-term activities that wake up the body and rejuvenate the cells. They put just enough strain on the body for just long enough to kill off the weak mitochondria (the brain of your cells) and empower the strong mitochondria. Like most forms of exercise, they are good enough to burn off your stress *in the right now.*

But if we want to get rid of stress from the past, then we need to add the deep body rest of meditation. Most forms of hormesis are brief, so that your body burns off stress chemicals in the moment so they don't become chronic. *It's not bad for your body to **get** stressed; however, it is toxic for your body to **stay** stressed.*

Unfortunately, the reflexive part of the human brain responsible for squirting out chemicals in response to high-stress situations can't distinguish between life-or-death demands and the stress of a pending deadline or a bad breakup. In other words, our brains react to most demands as if they were a tiger attack, even if they're not life-threatening. As a result, we're walking around our twenty-first-century lives with minds and bodies primed to ward off threats that are not a part of most people's daily experiences anymore—and the negative effects are quickly adding up.

We all know the feeling of being so stressed that we can't seem to think straight, complete a simple task without our hands shaking, or make a sound decision when the pressure is mounting. Now imagine if that were your default setting: having to function in high-demand, high-stakes situations day in and day out. Wait—that's already your reality, isn't it?

Even if we aren't always in panic mode as we watch the clock tick down, most of us are still living in a world of heightened anxiety and tension—yet we're still expected to react as if nothing's the matter. If you've ever felt overwhelmed by your inability to cope with all the demands on you, I want you to be gentle with yourself, because it's not your fault. Your brain and body are responding in the only way they know how. My goal is to give you an alternative—one that, over time, may just change the trajectory of your life.

Stress has been getting a bad rap these days. It gets blamed for high blood pressure and heart attacks; it's been called an epidemic—

the "Black Plague of our century."[1] And while I definitely don't disagree with these assessments and have committed my life to reversing the negative effects of stress, let's first understand why, over time, the human body has changed in the way it reacts to stress before we finish sharpening our pitchforks.

» De-Exciting the Nervous System

Back when you were either swinging a club to bludgeon that tiger or sprinting to your cave in hopes of outrunning it, your body was able to burn off those stress chemicals. In our far more sedentary modern life, however, our bodies need a different outlet to release that stress. This is why a lot of people say to me, "Exercise is my meditation." Actually, no. It's not. Exercise is exercise; meditation is meditation. They are different things, which is why they have their own words. What people usually mean when they say that exercise is their meditation is that physical exertion is an avenue for stress release, much as meditation is an avenue for stress release. To that end, exercise and meditation are similar, but they achieve that end in very different ways because they do very different things to our nervous systems.

When you exercise, you excite your nervous system and increase your metabolic rate. This is not to say that exercise doesn't help with stress release—it does. Exercise can help you get rid of stress from today. But when you meditate, you *de*-excite your nervous system, which decreases your metabolic rate, which helps you get rid of stress from your past. (Don't worry—this does *not* mean you'll gain weight if you meditate. Your metabolic rate is simply the rate at which your body consumes oxygen!)

When you de-excite your nervous system, you enable it to purge old stress from the body in a far more efficient manner, clearing the way for better performance and mental clarity. Have you ever tried to remove a piece of rice from a pot of boiling water? It's nearly impossible. But by simply removing the pot from the heat source for a few seconds and allowing the water molecules to calm from their agitated state, you can scoop out that tiny speck of rice with no issues.

Meditation allows you to rapidly de-excite the nervous system and give your body deep rest. This creates order in the nervous system so you can expel stress that is otherwise nearly impossible to remove. This is just one of the ways meditation makes you more productive.

In the previous chapter, I mentioned the corpus callosum, the thin strip of white matter that connects the gray matter of the two hemispheres of your brain. It is a bridge of nerve fibers that allows one side of the brain to communicate with the other side, carrying neural transmissions back and forth between the right and left brains to help facilitate the overall function of the mind. Neurobiologists have known for years that a meditator will have a thicker corpus callosum than a nonmeditator, but correlation does not necessarily equate to causation, so scientists were unable to confirm whether that strengthening of the nerve fibers was directly tied to the practice of meditation. Thanks to recent advances in neuroscience, we are able to see tangible proof that the brains of meditators are different, and that meditation actually changes the brain. The longer you have a daily meditation practice, the thicker the corpus callosum becomes.

In 2012, a team of neurologists at UCLA's Laboratory of Neuromodulation and Neuroimaging published a study that clearly demonstrated the thickening of the corpus callosum in people with regular meditation practices.[2] Even more interesting, in 2015, a team from Harvard published findings from an experiment in which they conducted baseline MRIs on participants before starting half of them on a regular, daily meditation program.[3] The subjects were selected on the basis of their overall health; all subjects, however, reported dealing with the effects of stress on their lives. During the course of the experiment, subjects answered questions about their moods and emotional states; those in the meditation group reported more positive overall feelings and a reduction of stress. At the end of eight weeks, the scans were repeated, and the brains of those who had begun meditating showed unmistakable physical changes, including shrinking of the amygdala (that is, the brain's fear center), which expands when the brain is steeped in cortisol or other stress hormones, and expansion of the brain stem, where dopamine and serotonin—the chemicals responsible for feelings of happiness, love, and contentment—originate.

Just think about that for a minute: *In only two months, meditation can change the brain enough to be visibly detectable by MRI,* shrinking the fear center and enlarging the centers responsible for happiness, love, and creative problem-solving.

Meditation, it turns out, is literally a mind-changing experience. The left brain is, in essence, in charge of the past and the future—reflecting on lessons learned and planning for what is ahead. It's in charge of language, critical thought, analytical thought, math, balancing your checkbooks, managing your responsibilities—all really important activities that make us act like functional adults. (Or at least a lot closer to the respectable people our parents desperately hoped we would grow up to become.) For most of us, and especially for high achievers, we've been taking our left brain to the gym day in and day out, working out to the same song: "Think, take action, achieve, and make money so you can be happy in the future." Your left brain is a total stud that never skips leg day.

Meanwhile, for most of us in modern Western society, our poor little right brains are in a state of near atrophy. The right brain is the piece of you that's in charge of the right now, of intuition, inspiration, creativity, music, and connectedness. The right brain is where our creative problem-solving epiphanies and our innovative approaches to common challenges come from. Unfortunately, the reason these flashes of brilliance are usually just that—short, temporary flashes where our right brain bursts onto the scene with some amazing stroke of genius and then fades back into the background—is that we've conditioned our left brain to be hypervigilant. The left brain often steps in and takes over before our right brain is done doing its thing.

If you look at a human brain, it's physically divided in half, with the size and shape of the right and left hemispheres perfectly balanced. I don't think Nature makes mistakes. *I don't believe Nature would have given us a 50/50 brain if we were supposed to use 90/10.* When we meditate, we are taking our brain to the gym to strengthen the corpus callosum, to reinforce and redouble the bridge between our left and right brains. This creates brain cohesion, meaning that the communication and interaction between the two hemispheres is increased.

What does this have to do with stress? Simply this: When you're in a high-demand situation, you can feel your body and mind beginning to descend into stressful responses. When you have a strong balance between your right brain and left brain, instead of slipping into fight-or-flight mode, you're going to find that your mind is able to remain clear, open, and capable of coming up with creative solutions. Your brain will be better equipped to resist a panicked response to a stressor, whether it's your boss yelling at you, a really tight deadline, or a competitor breathing down your neck, while simultaneously accessing a whole other realm of inspiration.

» The Artist Formerly Known as Stress

Contrary to popular belief, stress is not helping you in the productivity or performance department. In fact, according to the Vedas, ***"There is no such thing as a stressful situation, only stressful responses to a given situation."*** In other words, stress is not what happens to you; stress is your *reaction* to what happens to you.

When you become a meditation teacher, you become an expert on stress. Stress is at epidemic levels in the West, as well as in much of the rest of the world. But what do we really mean when we use the word *stress*?

Let's take a minute to discuss what stress is not: Stress is not deadlines, breakups, going to see your family at Thanksgiving, or your morning commute. All these things are *demands;* they are *demanding* your time and attention, and they are burning up your adaptation energy. For this reason, I have actually moved away from using the word *stress* to talk about all the pressures of our professional and personal responsibilities; instead, I prefer to call them demands. We juggle many demands on our time; our *stress* is the negative impact we allow those demands to have.

Every fast-food meal you've ever eaten, every Jack Daniel's you've ever drunk, every all-nighter you've ever pulled, every flight you've ever taken—all those things burn up your body's adaptation energy. They're not necessarily "bad," but they're all outside the basic norm our body and mind have evolved to be compatible with. They're affecting the way you handle stress right now, and this impacts the way you'll handle stress in the future. Here's the trick: If you have a bunch of demands that burn up your adaptation energy and then you have one *more* demand, your body is going to launch involuntarily into a fight-or-flight stress reaction. And that is what stress is: your reaction to the stuff, not the stuff itself.

ADAPTATION ENERGY: The body's ability to handle a change of expectation or a demand.

DEMAND: The artist formerly known as stress.

We don't act in accordance with what we know; we act in accordance with the baseline level of stress in our nervous systems. Hopefully this is comforting news, because it means you're *not* a failure if you didn't implement the lessons you've learned from every self-help book you've ever bought. The icing on the cake is that the technique you'll learn in this book will allow you to start running all the fancy software (information) you've acquired by defragging your hard drive (aka your brain).

This concept is foreign to most of us, so I want to put our new vocab words all together. If you're out of *adaptation energy* and you have another *demand,* your body will launch involuntarily into a fight-or-flight stress reaction, whether you have read *The Power of Now* or not. Meditation allows you to rapidly refill your reservoir of adaptation energy, which in turn gives you the luxury of choosing how you want to respond to life's demands. This may sound like a small benefit. It is not. Responding elegantly to demands rather than your body habitually flying off the handle can make the difference between heaven on earth or a living hell.

Let's take a moment to do a side-by-side comparison of the days of two hypothetical people we'll call Suzie Stressbox and Peggy Performer. Peggy has a twice-daily meditation practice; Suzie does not.

	Suzie Stressbox	Peggy Performer
6:00 A.M.	Exhausted from the day before, Suzie hits snooze on her alarm until 6:45.	Peggy wakes up before her alarm goes off, brushes her teeth, and settles in for her 15-minute meditation.
8:00 A.M.	Frantic because she's overslept, Suzie races to drop her daughter off at school. They are late and Suzie doesn't have time to grab coffee or breakfast—which she desperately needs.	Peggy packs herself a healthy lunch and gets her daughter dressed, fed, and off to school on time. She arrives at work a few minutes early.
11:00 A.M.	Suzie's boss changes the due date on a big project. Panicked because she's already behind, Suzie works through lunch to get it done.	Peggy's boss changes the due date on a project. She remains calm and uses creative problem-solving to get the job done in 90 minutes. She pauses her work to eat her lunch and enjoys a few minutes outside.
3:00 P.M.	Barely squeaking in before the deadline, Suzie turns in her project. Not having eaten all day and now behind on the day's work, Suzie runs to Starbucks for a coffee and a slice of banana bread.	Peggy uses a spare conference room for her afternoon meditation. Having filled up on adaptation energy and feeling refreshed, she dives into her tasks for the rest of the workday.
6:00 P.M.	Head pounding and ravenously hungry, Suzie hits traffic on the way home and angrily honks at the cars in front of her.	Sitting in traffic on her way home from work, Peggy listens to a favorite podcast and enjoys her extra time alone.

	Suzie Stressbox	Peggy Performer
8:00 P.M.	Suzie and her husband have a difficult conversation about his aging mother. Suzie breaks down in tears; it feels like too much to handle after a tough day.	Peggy and her husband discuss the health of his aging mother. Peggy listens compassionately, then she and her husband calmly work together to come up with solutions to this difficult situation.
8:30 P.M.	Suzie's daughter interrupts. With no patience left, Suzie snaps and yells at her daughter to get in bed and go to sleep.	Peggy's daughter interrupts. Peggy scoops her up, grateful for the joy she brings to their lives. Peggy reads her daughter a book before bed and kisses her good night.
10:00 P.M.	Suzie is mentally fried but stays up late working because she's frustrated with how little she accomplished today. She hopes tomorrow will be better.	Peggy puts down her book and reflects on how much she has to be grateful for. She feels proud of how she handled her high-demand day and looks forward to tomorrow.

» Your Relationship with Stress

What if, like Suzie Stressbox, you secretly crave that stress? Some of us wear our stress as a badge of honor. There is a little piece of us that enjoys how important it makes us feel or how in demand we are.

I teach a lot of CEO and actor types, and they have two different stories that both point to the same addiction. My CEO clients insist, "Emily, I need my stress. I need my angst. It's the thing that gives me my competitive edge." My actor clients insist, "Emily, I need my stress. I need my angst. My pain is where my creativity comes from."

Nope.

Your stress reactions are *not* the source of your inspiration, ingenuity, or vision. Your creativity and innovation come from the right hemisphere of your brain, not from any biological reaction designed to protect you from a predator. If the two hemispheres of your brain are able to communicate clearly and easily, you'll be better able to access your creative solutions and genius ideas even in the middle of a high-demand situation. Stress makes you stupid because it costs your brain and body so much energy preparing for something that isn't even real. When we meditate, we take that mental and physical energy back, allowing us to get more done in less time.

Let's do a little math experiment to evaluate how you are coping with your stress. Over the last six months, how much has stress cost you in:

Alcohol?
Therapy?
Coffee?
Cigarettes?
Binge shopping?
Anonymous sex?
Medications?
Recreational drugs?
Missed appointments?
Lost job opportunities?
Sick days?

When you stop to consider the actual toll stress is taking in terms of time, money, and self-respect, it seems unimaginable that you would *not* want to take steps to shed this pollutant from your system. I am going to give you a homework assignment at the end of this chapter where you will actually tally up the money and time wasted on stress. Accumulated stresses have been slowly seeping negativity and insecurity into your life like poisons, and because you're human, you seek outlets to feel better. The trick here is that lots of people stand to make lots of money off this fruitless search. The entire multibillion-dollar advertising industry is built on it.

Not only can meditation save you money in all the fruitless things you may have tried to curb your stress, but after it becomes a daily habit it may become invaluable to you. We give our Ziva grads an exit survey five months after they begin their journey, and one of the questions we ask is, "How much would you need to be paid to stop meditating entirely?" The average amount reported is $975 million! Granted, that is hardly a scientific study, and certainly impossible to objectively quantify, but it makes an important point all the same about how valuable finding your own happiness can be. (Personally, no amount of money could ever convince me to drop my daily practice, because I would just end up a really rich insomniac, and it's impossible to enjoy life when you're completely knackered!)

Before we move on, I want to make sure you take the time to do that assignment and figure out what stress is costing you in terms of time. It is so powerful to have before-and-after data. Most of us are terrible at recognizing and celebrating our successes, so I want to share a story with you from one of our zivaONLINE students, Shaunda Brown, who tested her cortisol levels before and after the training.

I started losing my hair and had bald spots at the age of thirty-five. While I consider myself healthy, I found out that I had alopecia areata due to high cortisol from stress. I always thought this stress was normal in the nonstop, busy life of growing a company, having an active social schedule, and what I had previously considered living my best life.

I decided to make some changes and reached out to Emily Fletcher for help. I started meditating regularly for fifteen minutes twice a day. It was so impactful that I immediately felt more present and able to handle important decisions with ease. I started sleeping better, became more efficient, got more accomplished, let go of things that had previously overwhelmed me, and stepped into what is truly my best life, with each day being better than before. My test results show the incredible difference Ziva has made to my body, with a *tenfold reduction in my stress.*

Before zivaONLINE my Na/Mg ratio (a measure of adrenal function) was very high—96. This indicates adrenal insufficiency. In my most recent test the Na/Mg level *dropped from 96 to 10,* indicating my stress levels and adrenal health have improved tenfold in only five months!

» Emotional Detox

Before I share the specific techniques you'll be using to meditate, it's important to take a moment to explore the process by which our bodies begin to rid themselves of stress. This emotional preparation is essential for reaping maximum benefits and establishing the healthiest and most productive relationship with the Z Technique. If we agree that accumulated stress in the body is slowing us down and that it makes sense to get rid of it so we can perform at the top of our game, the next question we must ask is . . . *where does the stress go?*

Meditation wrings you out like a sponge, so if you have some sadness inside, you may have some sad-flavored stress coming up and out when you first start practicing. The same is true for anger, resentment, insecurity, and on through a whole host of unpleasant emotions. I warn all my Ziva students that during the first two weeks following the course there are to be no quitting of jobs, no divorces, and no proposals. People usually laugh—until they experience firsthand how intense the feelings can be as the body and mind detox. The fact is, stress can have the same flavor on the way out as it does on the way in. And as much as I would love to wave a magic wand and have your lifetime of stress disappear in an instant, that's not the way Nature works. That old stress from the dog that barked in your face when you were four may create some feelings of anxiety as it is released.

I find it helpful to warn people that these uncomfortable sensations may come, but it does get better. There is no way around but through. And I'll be walking you through this emotional and physical detox process in the coming chapters. The best thing you can do in the first few weeks after starting the Z Technique is to schedule some extra rest and make sure you have a solid support team around you. Maybe start a meditation-book club with some friends or coworkers and begin this program together. It is so much easier to stay committed if you have support and accountability. *As with any detoxification process, like quitting smoking or fasting, the initial responses can be strong as our bodies and minds release stress that's accumulated over our lifetimes.*

Some students report feelings of sadness or anger over past traumas they thought they had moved beyond; others have found that they are overcome with urges to drastically change the direction of their lives; still others are confounded by the physical manifestations of catharsis, such as tears with no discernible cause, or very vivid dreams, nightmares, nausea, or fogginess. I am not writing this to scare you; I share this so you can go into this detox process with your eyes wide open and prepared to bravely move through discomfort if it arises.

All these reactions are completely normal, and they're usually most intense in the first few days and weeks. If you find yourself wanting to quit your job, take a walk. If you want to divorce your partner, take a nap. If you want to move, take a bath. If that doesn't work, reach out to a fellow meditator in the zivaTRIBE online community at facebook.com/groups/zivaTRIBE.

It's also very possible that you'll have few or no symptoms of emotional detox. I didn't when I first started, but I still got tremendous benefits from meditation (clearly). In other words, the detox and the benefits don't always correlate. Unfortunately, there's no easy way to predict how your body will react to the initial phases of unstressing. Simply being aware of the possibility of strong physical reactions, however, allows you to prepare yourself for what may come, and also reminds you that this, too, shall pass. Our theme song through the initial detox phase will be "Better Out Than In!"

UNSTRESSING: The process of a lifetime of accumu-lated stresses leaving the body. This period can last a few days to a few months.

EMOTIONAL CATHARSIS: The purging of deep emo-tions, resulting in psychological healing and sometimes physical relief.

Stress is a bully. Stress keeps your body and your mind trapped in a place of perpetual unrest, worry, and discontent; it keeps you on edge, feeling nervous, and always looking over your shoulder—exactly like a playground tyrant. Meditation allows you to feel safe enough for emotional release. It allows you to finally let go of the fear and the panic that can take control of your body and mind. Like a loving mother, meditation wraps you in her bosom and lets your nervous system know you now have access to your own bliss and fulfillment internally, which allows you to feel safe enough to let go of a lifetime of stress. I want to encourage you to stand up to that bully, even though doing so can be scary at first.

When a person begins a meditation practice, he or she is jump-starting the unstressing process. I urge my students to move bravely through the temporary discomfort. Discomfort is not the same thing as suffering. Suffering is intense and prolonged pain; discomfort is a short period of intense feeling as you move through a release. On the other side of that temporary discomfort, you emerge stronger and better equipped for the future. The emotional detox you may experience at the outset of this process is nothing more than your body finally letting go of the backlog of stresses you've been accumulating over your lifetime. That's not to say these responses are not real or valid or intense, but simply to recognize that they are on their way out. They ultimately lead to liberation from stress and its effects on your physical state as well as your mental acuity and performance.

If you feel prepared to tackle your demands with a fully engaged brain and to release the lifetime of stress in your body, despite some possible initial discomfort, then you're ready to begin this practice. Remember that this is a journey about up-leveling your life. As your stress is gradually released, you'll begin enjoying the space and energy it leaves behind for creativity, productivity, and even an increased IQ—up to 23 percent in some studies![4] Remember, stress makes you stupid.

Eyes-Open Exercise

What Is Stress Costing You?

I want to get really practical here. The question I asked above regarding how much stress costs you was not a hypothetical one. Now it's time to write it down. You will be so happy you have this information a few months into your meditation career.

Look over your past six months of expenses and make note of the ways that stress slows you down and drains your bank account. If there are other things I didn't list here, feel free to add them in.

Over the past six months, how much money have you spent on the following?

alcohol

therapy

coffee

cigarettes

binge shopping

anonymous sex

medications

recreational drugs

missed appointments

lost job opportunities

sick days

Now I'd like you to tally up what you think those outlets are costing you in terms of time (how much is your time worth, after all?) over a six-month period. Surveys among my students have revealed that the number comes out to almost $6,000—that's nearly $12,000 a year! Now take a moment to write down what you could do with that extra money. Take your dream vacation? Hire a personal trainer? Invest in your child's college fund? Does it seem worth it to exchange fifteen minutes twice a day for that money?

If your numbers are causing you to have a stress reaction, feel free to engage in this simple but enjoyable exercise for getting out of feeling overwhelmed: Breathe in through your nose and imagine you're smelling the scent of freshly baked cookies. Hold that breath for a moment, then exhale out through your mouth, imagining that you're blowing out birthday candles. Repeat this exercise for at least three breath cycles.

Ziva Case Study 2

How I Stopped Being a "Meditation Failure"
MALCOLM FRAWLEY, REAL ESTATE DEVELOPER

My teen years were spent stuffing feelings into a metaphorical box so that no one, not even I, could see them. If I was sad, I would fake a smile; if I was angry, I would brush it off as if it were nothing. These habits grew into extreme behaviors in which I would withdraw fully from uncomfortable situations and have rash reactions to others. I was so out of touch with my own feelings that I made huge life decisions because of feelings *I didn't even know I was having.*

I spent the majority of my twenties on antidepressants, antianxiety medication, and sleeping pills. Countless therapists tried to "fix" me, but I was so out of touch with my own feelings that I wasn't sure what they were trying to fix.

After years of being medicated and eager to wean myself off my addiction to sleeping pills, I sought out alternatives. Meditation had just started becoming mainstream, and it was so exciting to be able to download an app that promised to make me feel better instantly. I would listen to certain mindfulness exercises and attempt to follow their directions. I would work to focus on my breath and "quiet my mind," but I could never quite understand how to do this. When the drop-in meditation studios began popping up, I thought, *This is my chance to learn how to stop my thoughts and finally find that bliss that everyone speaks of!* Unfortunately, that's not what I got. I found myself yet again getting told to sit up straighter, focus on my breathing, and stop thoughts from entering my mind. This only magnified my anxiety, in the very chair that was supposed to relax me, and left me thinking that "meditation" could now be added to the list of things I had tried and failed.

Later, in a discussion with a friend, I explained my failed attempts at meditating, and she suggested that

I might be doing the wrong *kind* of meditation. I didn't even know there were different kinds! She started raving about Emily and Ziva and all the amazing ways her life had changed because of it. I immediately got myself into Emily's next "Intro to Meditation" talk and was so inspired as she spoke about her personal experience of overcoming insomnia and how her life, as a whole, had changed for the better. I decided immediately that I had to learn.

Nine months later, I am incredibly happy to report that my life has changed in exactly the ways Emily said it might. For the first time in ten years, I am medication-free! I fall asleep effortlessly—without any kind of sleep aid—and wake up feeling rested and refreshed. But most important, I now connect with my own feelings. I can identify what comes up, feel it, and move on. My reactions are authentic to each moment, and I'm not stuck in the past reviewing old traumas. I'm now in a healthy, committed relationship in which I'm able to show up fully as myself. I'm more focused in my work and find creative outlets all over my life.

SLEEPLESS IN SEATTLE—AND
EVERYWHERE ELSE

LIFE SUCKS WHEN YOU'RE TIRED.

More than 40.6 million Americans—that's more than one-third of the adult population—have some trouble sleeping at night, according to the CDC. These issues range from restlessness to severe clinical insomnia. For some people, insomnia looks like lying in bed, fighting to go to sleep while lists from the day and plans for tomorrow rattle around in their brains. For other people, insomnia means having trouble going to bed at all, instead spending their nighttime hours puttering around the house or scrolling through social media because they can't get their brain and body to power down together. And for still others, insomnia is a series of short bouts of almost falling asleep before suddenly being pulled out of it because the lyrics from their fourth-grade chorus recital suddenly rise to the surface and refuse to be quieted. There are countless other ways that sleeplessness can present itself, and they're all maddening.

When I was "living my dream" on Broadway, every night became a battle for me to fall asleep. Every night as I tried to sleep, some combination of anxiety, screwed-up circadian rhythm, and adrenaline from that night's performance pumped through my body. I would lie in bed for hours, wide awake yet desperate for rest, knowing every minute that passed would leave me that much more exhausted the next day, when I was expected to perform at the top of my game.

A recent study out of Canada found that people who regularly clocked fewer than six hours of sleep per night suffered from acute impairment in their reasoning and perception, and that the long-term effects of sleep deprivation were akin to those of chronic binge drinking.[1] The same study noted that "driving while sleep deprived . . . is the cognitive impairment equivalent of drunk driving." Is that really what you want as the norm for your life—drunk driving through your day?

We all know that decent sleep is important for physical and mental health. Some of the top NBA players sleep as much as twelve hours a night to rejuvenate. Our parents have drilled that into us since we were kids, first when we started fighting naps as toddlers, and later when we were begging to stay up later to read one more chapter or watch one more show. Did our parents have a self-serving agenda, needing us to go to bed for their own sanity? Most definitely—but that doesn't mean they weren't right. Daytime clarity, workplace productivity, longevity, a strengthened immune system, even weight loss—these are all proven benefits of an adequately rested mind and body. And yet even though we all understand the vital importance of sleep, what's the first place we tend to cut corners when faced with an extra-full schedule? You guessed it—our sleep. We go to bed later, get up earlier, pull all-nighters, and rely on caffeine, energy drinks, or whatever else is available to keep ourselves awake and grind through the day, then barely rest before doing it all over again the next day. I know I've been guilty of it, and there's no doubt you have, too. Why do we continue to do this to ourselves when we know better?

We live in a *go-go-go!* world that tends to equate resting with laziness, even though we can get much more accomplished at a much higher level in much less time if we approach each day thoroughly rested. We all know it, yet we still think we can somehow beat the system. I have news for you: *Nature is a perfect accountant.* It's sort of like a casino: You can try to cheat the house—and you may even get ahead for a little while—but in the end, the house always wins. You can't short yourself of two hours of sleep per night and expect your body not to notice. In one month, that comes out to more than fifty-six hours of missed sleep. Think about that. If you go to bed one hour later and get up one hour earlier than you should for one month, you're shortchanging your body almost *two and a half full days' worth* of rest.

Plenty of my meditation students tell me their jam-packed schedules don't allow for a full eight hours of sleep every night. For the sake of argument, I can accept that, but there is something everyone can do to create deeper, more efficient sleep in the time you *do* have. Care to take a guess at what that thing is?

» Sleep vs. Meditation

Scientists used to believe that the brain and body both powered down when a person went to sleep. It wasn't until the 1950s, when neural imaging became more advanced, that researchers were able to trace how the body and brain interact while seemingly at rest all night.

A normal adult will experience 90- to 110-minute cycles of sleep stages throughout the course of the night. Hooked up to that normal adult's brain, a scanner will show what looks like a series of hills and valleys as the person's mental activity rises and falls in predictable patterns during sleep, depending on whether the person is in a light sleep, deep sleep, or rapid eye movement (REM) sleep. Scientists have classified these phases of brain activity into various types of "waves."

As soon as you drift off, eye movement decreases and the brain shifts from its conscious, waking state into one where it produces slower alpha and theta waves. After anywhere from one to ten minutes, the brain suddenly produces a surge of oscillatory brain activity called sleep spindles or sigma bands before slowing down drastically. As you sink into a deeper sleep, the body becomes far less responsive to external stimuli, eye and muscle movement all but stop, and your brain continues to produce slow delta waves until you move into REM sleep. This is the stage during which you may have your most vivid dreams. Your eyes move rapidly despite being closed, and your heart rate and blood pressure both elevate. REM sleep can last for up to an hour before your brain pulls you back up to stage 1 and the sleep cycle begins again. Although scientists still do not fully understand why the brain and body react to sleep as they do, they do know that each of the deeper stages of sleep has various benefits, such as repairing muscles and healing injuries, converting new information in the brain into memories, and processing the previous day's events.

This shallow-deep-shallow cycle is repeated throughout the night in a near universal pattern among healthy adults living amid the mainstream demands of the industrialized world. Interestingly, however, sleep studies conducted on meditators show that their brains tend to advance quickly through the initial stages from light to deep sleep and then stay in the deeper states until morning.

When you sleep, your mind continues to process information it gathers from your day, which is why we often have stress dreams during particularly demanding times or nightmares after watching scary movies. The brain is filtering through all its recent input and aligning it with the long-term beliefs and structures present in your subconscious. As we already discussed, stress escapes the body in

Sleep Before Ziva

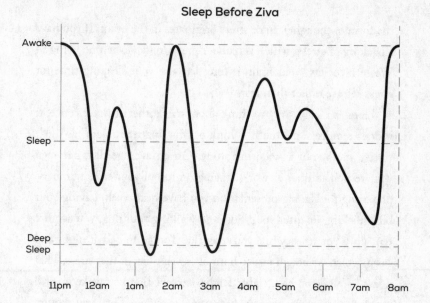

Sleep 3 Days After Starting Ziva

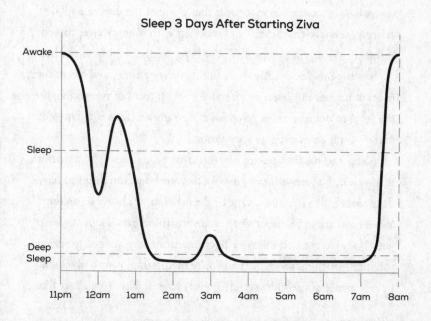

the form of thoughts, since stress originates in the brain. If you have a backlog of stress, which is true for pretty much everyone living in Western society, your brain is forced to use your sleeping time for stress release rather than rest.

Here's a clearer way to think about this rather abstract concept; it does require some math. Think of this "math problem" as illustrative math, not a scientific study. On an average day, between your responsibilities at work, staying on top of your sales numbers, preparing for the big presentation you have next week, paying your bills, picking up after your kids, and walking your dog, you acquire ten "units" of stress while you're awake. You go to bed at night and sleep, which is enough rest to burn off seven units of that stress. That doesn't sound too bad, right? Right—except that you wake up still carrying three units of stress from the day before. Then you acquire ten units of stress that day, which means you're now carrying thirteen units. You go to sleep that night, release seven units—and wake up with six. Acquire ten more over the course of the day for a total of sixteen, sleep, release seven, and wake up with nine, twelve, fifteen, eighteen. Wash, rinse, repeat. You've been doing this your entire life.

See the problem? This stress builds up over time, and sleep, for most of us, has not been an effective enough form of rest to handle the level of demand most of us have been under. This is what leads many people to investigate meditation.

Sleep and meditation are not the same type of rest. As a matter of survival, Nature will not allow both your body and mind to have deep rest at the same time. One or the other must always be on duty. When you are in blackout sleep, your breathing gets deeper to keep your body oxygenated in case a tiger pounces and you need to spring into fight-or-flight mode. When you're meditating, your body is able to rest while your brain stands guard; this is why it can feel like you become hyperaware during meditation—your brain is staying alert so you don't become a tiger snack. ***Sleep is rest for your brain; meditation is rest for your body.*** You need to have both to thrive, and meditation allows you to do both more effectively. Hee Sun-Woo, a producer in New York City, wrote to me and shared, "I slept through the night for the first time in twenty years after following your methods." It was a simple shift in his daily routine that paid dividends in rest.

» The Fourth State

The three states of consciousness most of us are familiar with are waking, sleeping, and dreaming. However, in recent years, scientists, sleep specialists, and other experts have conducted more than 350 peer-reviewed studies whose results were published in more than 160 scientific journals, and the findings all pointed toward the same conclusion: There are more than three states of consciousness, and meditation is one means of accessing these states.

I call the fourth state "the bliss field"; the more common term for this state is *transcendence,* but that word has accumulated a lot of different associations and baggage. The original term is *turiya,* a Sanskrit word for "the fourth" or a state of pure consciousness, wholeness, or union with the source.

TURIYA: A hypometabolic state of "restful alertness"; the state of consciousness, unique from waking, sleeping, or dreaming, you enter when practicing *nishkam karma* meditation. When you are in this state, much of the brain lights up in scans, as opposed to when you are in mindfulness or directed-focus practices, where a smaller portion of the brain lights up but is very bright.

You know that feeling when you're just drifting off to sleep but are still conscious? Think of that mental place as a hallway. If you pass through one door, you'll end up sleeping; if you pass through another, you enter *turiya*. Both destinations lead you to a place of rest, but in one case, it's rest for the body, and in the other, it's rest for the brain. It's actually quite simple, except that we rarely think about the difference between such similar-feeling but vastly different modes of consciousness.

Meditation is like giving a gift to your body—a chance to take some time off instead of requiring it to always stand guard ready to launch into fight or flight to protect your brain and keep you alive while you sleep. When you meditate, your body can stand down and release accumulated stress while your brain becomes hyperconscious.

» Meditation Is the New Caffeine

In case you missed it, meditation takes only half an hour out of your day, but it helps relieve you of roughly the same amount of stress as a full night's sleep. Mathematically, that doesn't seem possible, but remember that sleep and meditation are vastly different forms of rest.

The state of consciousness achieved in meditation is anywhere from two to five times deeper than sleep. By this estimation a fifteen-minute meditation is roughly equivalent to a sixty-minute nap; completing two fifteen-minute meditations is like giving yourself an extra two hours of sleep. Additionally, because you're resting your body rather than your mind, your brain can prioritize intense de-stressing and repairing the body during meditation. You know that feeling when you go into the office on a Saturday, when no one else is in the building—or maybe you just turn off your phone and your e-mail alerts so there are no interruptions clamoring for your attention? It's a completely different sense of accomplishment and efficiency, all because you don't have twenty other things pulling you off task while you're trying to work.

In chapter 10, we'll discuss exactly how meditation allows your brain to more readily notice subtle differences and detect patterns and themes, which is one of the things that makes you more productive. You can't eliminate demands from your life, but you can take steps to train your mind to better adapt to whatever comes your way.

And the icing on the meditation cake? You come out of your meditation more alert. There is no "nap hangover" as you try to wake up *because you never went to sleep in the first place*. Your brain releases bliss chemicals during meditation, not sleep chemicals.

This is also the reason I like to refer to meditation as "the new caffeine." A lot of people—maybe even most people—use caffeine as a substitute for sleep or as a productivity tool. Need to get moving in the morning? Grab a cup of coffee. Need a pick-me-up in the afternoon? Swig a caffeinated soft drink. All you really need is caffeine, right? Wrong. What you really need is *rest*.

It's true that caffeine makes you *feel* more awake, but not because it gives you deep rest. You feel more awake because caffeine masks the brain's ability to feel tired.

I used to think that caffeine was nothing more than a mild stimulant that bumped up the nervous system to a slightly higher level, which was the reason it made everyone more productive. But it's not as simple as that. Caffeine is molecularly similar to a chemical called adenosine, which is the hormone your brain produces throughout the day that makes you feel sleepy and cues you to go to bed when your body is ready.[2] When caffeine is ingested, it actually blocks your brain's adenosine receptors, which means your brain can't tell you're tired. That's the reason you're able to accomplish more after a dose or two of caffeine. That may sound good, but caffeine is really just hijacking your nervous system.

Now, blocking those receptors in your brain is not bad for you in and of itself—that is to say, it's not hurting you while it's happening. But when the caffeine wears off and leaves those adenosine receptors open, all the adenosine your brain has been producing while you were rocking your caffeine high comes flooding in. This is what creates the crash and leaves you reaching for a second, third, or fourth cup. As John Mackey, CEO of Whole Foods, says, if you're reliant on caffeine, your energy is not your own.

Caffeine *synthetically* stimulates neural activity in the brain. When your pituitary gland notices this increase in neural activity, it thinks there's some sort of an emergency happening, so it triggers your adrenal glands to start releasing adrenaline. Since adrenaline is the number one stress chemical that gets released when you launch into a fight-or-flight stress reaction, caffeine is putting your body into mild crisis mode, and with it comes all those jittery side effects we discussed back in chapter 1. In short, caffeine artificially excites the nervous system.

I want to be very clear here: I am not saying you should never drink coffee again—I actually enjoyed a cup or two of Bulletproof coffee myself in the writing of this book. I just want you to make informed decisions about any mind-altering substance you put in your body. If the pros outweigh the cons for you, then enjoy. But don't kid yourself into thinking that caffeine is *giving* you energy. It's not.

Can caffeine make you more productive? Sure. But it's only a temporary boost. That's why meditation is such a superior alternative. Rather than looking to external sources and ultimately depleting your adrenals, it provides a sustainable and renewable *resource of energy within yourself* for as long as you continue your twice-daily practice. Like caffeine, meditation will make you more productive, but it does so in a very different way: through a form of rest that is exponentially deeper than sleep, and in a manner that de-excites (rather than stimulates) your nervous system.

When you allow your mind and body to become more naturally in sync, you can decrease (or even eliminate) the amount of synthetic stimulation you previously required in order to feel fully awake and productive. Because you're not masking your brain's request for sleep but are instead developing an ability to rest more effectively, you're setting yourself up for much more productivity in the long run. By stopping the biological depletion cycle that has become the norm in our culture and replacing it with a self-sufficient means of elevating your personal and professional performance, you're laying the groundwork for a more engaged, creative, rested, and healthy version of yourself to emerge.

Imagine a world where meditation stations are more common than coffee shops!

Ziva Case Study 3

Insomnia No More

AMBER SHIRLEY, FINANCIAL ADVISER

To say that I had a troubled relationship with sleep before I began my meditation practice would be an understatement. I would stay up late knowing I had to be up early. I convinced myself that anxiously replaying my day over something I said or didn't say was how I processed things.

I would doze off, only to wake up in varying degrees of anxiety a few hours later. In the middle of the night, I got my second wind. Wide awake, I would begin piddling around my apartment, checking e-mails, reading, showering. By the time I finally got to bed in the early morning hours, I was frustrated with myself, knowing I only had a few hours of sleep ahead of me.

With the buzz of my alarm, eyes half open, I'd groggily survey the scene: my bed in shambles, pillows strewn on the floor, my body in a completely different location from where I had begun the night. Every morning I woke up feeling more tired than I'd felt when I went to bed the night before.

Working with Emily's techniques changed everything.

Now my sleep is so intensely deep that I have to set myself up for success before I even get into bed: The lights must already be turned off, my sheets pulled back, and my body positioned in just the right spot. Why? you ask. I now fall asleep so quickly and so deeply that wherever I land is where I stay until morning. When I wake up, it looks as if no one was even in the bed.

I had heard miraculous stories of people curing their insomnia overnight. I eagerly anticipated the surge of energy and clarity I heard friends describe after beginning meditation.

That was not my immediate experience.

I couldn't believe how exhausted I was. I was irritable,

my body ached, and I fought to stay awake more than three hours at a time. Each day I would walk in and take my seat, and within thirty minutes, I'd be knocked out. I basically slept through the entire course and then some. Thankfully, I was off from work that week and able to luxuriate in a sixteen-hour-a-day sleep schedule.

But this was not the magical experience I had signed up for. Where was my surge of energy and clarity? What about my damn bliss? I remember going up to Emily after one of the classes and asking, "Why am I sleeping for sixteen hours straight? I can't do this forever—I have a job. I have a life."

What I was experiencing was the unstressing that Emily had spoken about. It was intense. My short temper and fatigue made even my mom question whether meditation was a good fit for me.

Within a week and a half of twice-a-day Ziva time, I was sleeping a solid eight hours. The following month, I found myself naturally going to bed earlier and waking up much, much earlier. I'm talking bright-eyed and bushy-tailed, refreshed and ready to greet the day hours before my alarm clock went off. In fact, I didn't use an alarm for the next three years. I was sleeping only four to six hours a night and experiencing sustained and focused energy all day long. When I would feel a slight dip in energy late in the afternoon, it was my body telling me it was time for my second meditation.

Now, five years into my twice-daily sittings, I need about eight hours a night in the winter months and only four to six hours in warm weather. I rarely feel tired.

Meditation has given me the freedom to enjoy the kind of deep rest that can only be experienced with a relaxed nervous system. My well-rested nervous system has trained my body how to receive and integrate energy from sources other than sleep: sunlight, nourishing foods, quiet time, inspiring conversations, and meaningful connections.

Sleep was just the beginning of my meditation life upgrade. Getting to the chair twice a day every day has shown me how to show up more fully and authentically in every area of my life. Meditation has given me the clarity and confidence to make big strides in my career and positively transform my relationships with family, friends, and money. Sharing the gift of meditation is one of my favorite things.

SICK OF BEING SICK

I USED TO THINK IT WAS NORMAL TO GET SICK THREE OR FOUR times a year; every season change would find me commiserating with my friends about the nasty new bug that was going around. I even had to get my tonsils removed in college because the severe sore throats I kept getting were interfering with my singing.

That all changed the day I learned meditation. Once I began meditating twice a day, I did not get sick again for eight and a half years! That's right—I skipped anywhere from twenty-four to thirty-two total illnesses during that time. Not a cold, not a flu, hardly even a sniffle before my immune system would come to the rescue. (In fact, when I did finally get sick, almost nine years later, it was the night after my bachelorette party, so I feel I earned that one.)

What about you? How many times a year do you come down with something? How much does that cost you in time away from work, missed opportunities, delayed deadlines, and self-imposed quarantine from family?

» Prevention and Healing

Nature didn't intend for us to be sick, tired, and stressed most of the time; in fact, our bodies are equipped with a powerful internal pharmacy designed to keep us healthy. However, stress can overwhelm our bodies and prevent our immune systems from running optimally. When you use your daily Z Technique as a time for stress release, you can use your sleep as a time for sleep. If your brain is not so busy running stress-removing functions during sleep, it has more energy available for immune function. In short, meditation helps get you out of a chronic low-grade fight-or-flight response that puts your immune system on the back burner while your body prepares for an imaginary predatory attack. Once your body realizes there are no large cats lurking nearby, it can convert that wasted energy into an optimal immune response to whatever illnesses you may be facing.

The immune system can be activated by a lot of different things: viruses, bacteria, even the overproduction of mutated cells that lead to cancer. Setting aside time for meditation can calm your nervous system and reinvigorate your immune system so it's ready to act when you need it. This is good news for your daily life, of course, because no one actually likes getting sick. A healthier you also has a positive impact on your professional and creative life, because your mind is agile, your body is functioning as it was designed to, and you aren't missing work, meetings, calls with clients, or other important responsibilities.

You perform better when you're not sick. I know this sounds incredibly obvious, but just because we know intuitively that something is the best course doesn't mean we always follow through on it. We have all sorts of means of keeping ourselves well, from avoiding handshakes to bathing in hand sanitizer, but if you keep falling ill regardless, it's worth considering adding another proactive and precautionary measure to your toolbox. I had the honor of teaching a group of physicians and Ph.D. researchers at one of the world's top hospitals, and the results were extraordinary. Many other hospital groups look to their example, so my hope is that we can start to give doctors more tools to handle their own extraordinary stress levels so they can confidently start to prescribe meditation as frequently as medication. I have had a number of physicians follow my methods, and one of them wrote afterward:

> *If I could prescribe one thing to every single patient who walks in my door it would be this: Learn a daily meditation practice. It will change your life. It literally rewires the brain, calms the nervous system, and creates new neural pathways via plasticity mechanisms. It lowers stress hormones (like adrenaline and cortisol), lowers heart rate and blood pressure, decreases inflammation, increases focus, and makes you feel centered and grounded, to name just a few benefits. You can do it anywhere and it requires a very small chunk of time with massive results.*

Meditation does more for the body than helping to ramp up your immune system and stave off illness, though; it can actually *promote* healing on a cellular level.

In 2004, Japanese researcher Dr. Masaru Emoto released *The Hidden Messages in Water*. His book, which quickly became a *New York Times* bestseller, used microscopic photography to document differences in the formation of ice crystals between water that had been exposed to positive attention, water that had been regularly exposed to negative attention, and a control group. These samples showed distinctions similar to a second experimental group that compared water that came from unpolluted springs and water drawn from contaminated sources. The water molecules that were surrounded by "good" (energetically clean) environments were neatly ordered when viewed under a microscope, and formed beautiful ice crystals; the water that had been surrounded by "bad" (energetically toxic) environments were chaotic under the microscope, and formed ice crystals in far less visually pleasing shapes. Dr. Emoto concluded that if external factors as seemingly abstract as "positive attention" could visibly affect the molecular appearance of water—and given that the average adult human body is anywhere from 50 to 65 percent water—depending on gender and fitness (fat holds less water than muscle) it stands to reason that the external factors and energy that surround us have a similar impact on our physical well-being.

Apply these findings to how our bodies react to being flooded with the stress chemicals adrenaline and cortisol all the time, and you can imagine what kind of memory our cells are carrying. If you begin a daily practice, however, you will be flooding your body with dopamine and serotonin instead, allowing your body to rest—and ultimately heal—on a cellular level.

I must emphasize at the outset that I am not claiming meditation can cure any diseases, and if you're taking any medication or undergoing treatment for a medical condition, absolutely speak with your healthcare provider before making any changes, no matter how good meditation makes you feel. What meditation can do, however, is work alongside your medical care to supplement and strengthen your body's ability to heal any ailments you may be dealing with.

» Just What the Ayurvedic Doctor Ordered

The long-term effects of adrenaline and cortisol are no joke. For a start, both are highly acidic (remember that whole thing about your body wanting to taste nasty in case the tiger bites you?). It's all connected to a brilliant system of defense—brilliant, but harsh on the body if the stress is chronic. In fact, much of our Western lifestyle creates a highly acidic environment within our nervous system, organs, and tissues. The typical Western diet, for example, contains a lot of grain-fed meat; the stomach needs to produce extra acid in order to successfully break down that much animal protein, especially when the animal was raised on a diet that Nature did not design. Even the way we tend to approach exercise—pushing ourselves to the brink in an hour-long cardio class or maximizing our weight and reps to the point of exhaustion or muscle failure—creates a tremendous buildup of lactic acid within the body. This stands in stark contrast to many forms of exercise more commonly practiced in the East (consider yoga, tai chi, qigong, and so on), which tend to be more focused on gentle movement, breathwork, and stretching the body without creating extra internal "heat," aka acid. All this acid can lead to inflammation throughout the body, and according to Ayurvedic medicine and an increasing number of Western doctors, inflammation is the root of all chronic disease.

Ayurvedic medicine is one of the oldest systems of healing in the world, dating back more than three millennia. It takes a holistic approach to healing the body through food, exercise, and meditation and is rooted in the philosophy that you can be your own doctor if you learn and understand the laws of Nature and how your body, food, and exercise interplay with those laws. In Ayurvedic tradition, every action is either bringing you into balance or pulling you out of balance. Disease is inflammation—truly *dis-ease* of the body, in which certain elements are out of balance due to inflammation. Ayurvedic medicine is designed to bring all the elements back into balance to help you become vibrant and healthy while realizing your full human potential. *Ayur* means "longevity" and *veda,* as we discussed earlier, simply means "knowledge."

Ayurveda, therefore, means "knowledge of longevity." Ayurvedic medicine is concerned with not only treating sickness but optimizing health and performance through meditation, breathwork, diet, and exercise.

AYURVEDA: *Veda* means "knowledge." *Ayur* means "longevity." So *Ayurveda* is the "knowledge of longevity" or the knowledge of life; one of the world's most sophisticated and powerful systems of healing. More than a way of treating sickness, Ayurveda is about optimizing health and bringing the body into harmony with its environment.

AYURVEDIC MEDICINE: An ancient body of knowledge focused on a holistic approach to bringing all the elements of the body into balance. It is designed to help you become vibrant and healthy while realizing your full human potential.

Making consciously smarter decisions about what we eat, when we eat, and how active we are is nothing new; most of us know what we *should* be doing. But most of us *aren't* doing it. So how can this book help? In addition to the psychological benefits of starting your day with a healthy habit (making it so much easier to continue on that path and adopt additional healthy habits), the bliss chemicals dopamine and serotonin, which are produced only a few seconds into your meditation practice, are alkaline in nature; their mere presence in the body helps to neutralize some of the acid. In other words, meditation is a way to biologically counteract the acid in your body by making it more alkaline. It's better living through chemistry, at the most basic and organic level.

By practicing the 3 M's twice a day every day, you decrease the stress stored in your body, which allows your immune system to function as it is meant to and therefore decreases your susceptibility to illness. This will be your new foundation, but there are also some additional steps you can take to stay healthy throughout the year. Following is a list of some of my favorite "health hacks":

BLACK PEPPER TEA: This is an interesting trick my Ayurvedic doctor recommended, and I have used it with great results. When you're feeling under the weather, or if it's cold outside and you want to stave off illness, you can make this simple "tea" by boiling water, pouring it into your favorite mug, and adding five or six grinds of organic black pepper. Let all the pepper settle to the bottom of the mug, then drink the water; leave the pepper at the bottom of the mug. The pepper will induce a mild fever and help you sweat out the cold. Do this every two to three hours until your symptoms cease. (Pro tip: It's best to have black pepper tea with food, as it may cause nausea on an empty stomach. Feel free to add your favorite tea as well—I love Celestial Seasonings' Bengal Spice.)

OREGANO OIL: Put a few drops of oregano oil in the back of your throat when you're sick. Its natural antibacterial and antiviral properties can help knock out a cold or flu if you catch it early enough.[1] *Caution!* Oregano oil is very strong, so don't let it touch your lips or it may burn. (I imagine the burning sensation killing any unwanted pathogens on its way down.)

GARLIC: You may already have a super-easy natural remedy sitting in your kitchen: garlic. Garlic has antiviral and antibacterial properties and can be used for a wide range of ailments. You can eat a clove or chop it into pieces and swallow them like a pill to find relief from cold symptoms or to ward off infection.

CUCUMBER AND MINT: These are simple ingredients you can add to your diet to "cool" your body naturally by decreasing acidity and increasing alkalinity. These are prominent tools for changing the pH of the body in an Ayurvedic diet. They are cooling foods that also have detoxifying properties and can lower the level of acid or "heat" in the body.

ZINC GLUCONATE SPRAY, ELDERBERRY SYRUP, and high doses of **VITAMIN D** are also great ways to boost your immune system. (Be sure to check with your doctor before starting any new supplement, and know that the quality of the supplement matters.)

While meditation offers you a way to improve your health on multiple fronts, these Ayurvedic tips may prove helpful to you in combating bacterial or viral illnesses. The trick here is to remember that in the case of meditation, "maximum" is not synonymous with "optimum."

» Can I Meditate More Than Twice a Day?

Short answer: No. As you'll learn in the coming chapters, the Z Technique is a specific prescription of fifteen minutes two times a day, no more, no less. This is going to be your new norm 99 percent of the time. I lay out the exceptions below; what these exceptions have in common is that they involve an increase in *physical* demand.

EXTRA MEDITATION WHEN TRAVELING: It is not natural to wake up on one continent and go to sleep on another. It's not "bad," but when you change time zones, you really call on your body's ability to adapt; the same is true when you move at a faster speed than Nature intended (that is, as fast as you can walk or run on your own two feet). The result is jet lag. We've all experienced it, and we all know what a drag it can be when you're on the road for work and struggle just to make it through those first few days; by the time you've adjusted and are ready to perform at your peak, it's time to pack up and head home—and your best self never even got a chance to shine.

Amazingly, jet-lag reduction is one of the most commonly cited side benefits among Ziva graduates. Student reports (as well as my own personal experiences) indicate that meditation reduces the effects of jet lag to the point of virtually eradicating them. Because your body is able to more easily rid itself of that additional stress from high demand and replenish its supply of adaptation energy, which was burned off so rapidly while you were traveling, it's able to more quickly adapt and acclimatize to your new environment.

Anytime the human body moves faster than it can run, it burns up adaptation energy. Throw in dehydration, EMF radiation, recycled air, and exposure to countless germs from your fellow travelers, and flying is a perfect storm of sickness just waiting to happen.

Air travel can easily cause or aggravate illness. To combat these additional demands, I recommend you meditate more on travel days. Experiment with the program that follows to see what works best for you.

For a five- to six-hour flight, add two extra fifteen-minute meditations, for a total of four that day. I recommend completing one at takeoff and one at landing. If you have travel anxiety, you can simply meditate before boarding and before landing. It's not the timing that's crucial; it's the very act of meditating more frequently. For a short flight (one to three hours), only one extra meditation is needed. If you're on a long-haul flight (any flight longer than six hours), add one meditation for each five to six hours of time in the air. Do this every time you fly, and you'll notice a marked difference in the way your body reacts to air travel. (For other types of travel, such as road trips, train rides, and multiday cruises, add one extra meditation per day of travel.)

EXTRA MEDITATION WHEN YOU'RE SICK: Just as you can do more meditation when traveling because there's an increase in physical demand, you can also change the rules when you're sick. If you feel a cold or other illness coming on, add an extra sitting. Giving your body this additional rest will help boost immune function and help you heal. Ideally you incorporate the additional meditation time as soon as you notice that little tickle in the back of your throat, but if you've already confirmed with your doctor that you're full-on sick, you can meditate as much as is comfortable; let your body dictate how long and how often. You'll know you're doing too much if you get really emotionally sensitive and find it hard to perform daily tasks.

» Meditation vs. Medication

Migraines. Anxiety. Depression. Infertility. Adrenal fatigue. IBS. Insomnia. These are just a few of the ailments a regular, twice-daily practice can help abate.

I know at this point I must sound like a used-car salesman as I rattle off all the different ailments meditation can ease, but the question shouldn't be *"How can meditation help with so many things?"* but *"How can stress mess up so many things?"* To that end, I'd like to take a look at some of the conditions that meditation has been scientifically proven to help treat, as well as some that, while I can't provide any scientific evidence to confirm, Ziva students have consistently reported as improved with regular practice.

It is essential to remember I am not a physician and cannot encourage you to decrease your dosage of or eliminate any prescribed medications or other medical treatments. I have had a significant number of students who have found that a regular daily practice helped lessen certain symptoms, and I have worked with their healthcare providers when both patient and doctor were in a place where they felt they would like to try a lower dosage or a gradual weaning off a certain medication. *However, this was always under very tightly controlled and supervised circumstances, and only after the doctor was consulted and agreed to the plan.* No matter how much improvement you perceive in your health, always consult your healthcare provider before making any changes to your course of treatment.

BURNOUT AND CHRONIC FATIGUE

Burnout and chronic fatigue are epidemic today, and many Ziva practitioners—including me—suffered from one or both before beginning a meditation practice. By easing the body out of a chronic fight-or-flight state, the brain and the stress-response systems of the body are very often able to recover and resume healthy function. I took various herbs and adrenal supplements toward the end of my Broadway career because my adrenals were shot. After about a year of regular meditation practice, as my body's ability to regulate itself got stronger, I found I didn't need them anymore.

DEPRESSION AND ANXIETY

Different sides of the same coin, depression and anxiety both stem from a chemical imbalance triggered (in part) by an overdevelopment of the left brain. The right brain is in charge of the present, while the left brain reviews the past or rehearses the future. Depression replays the "would have/could have/should have" tapes of the past; anxiety locks onto the uncertainty and unpredictability of the future.

Meditation, as we have already discussed, helps you gain the tools you need to be more strongly rooted in the right now. For sufferers of depression and anxiety, meditation can be a means of helping to reframe and release a constant strain of unpleasant memories or fearful anticipation. By incorporating meditation into a wellness plan that also includes healthy changes to diet, exercise, sleep, and often some kind of counseling or therapy, I have had countless students report that their symptoms were greatly diminished or disappeared altogether.

It's important to remember, however, that the emotional detox process is a very real stage early in the journey. If you struggle with depression, anxiety, or any other type of mental health challenge, I urge you to consult with a healthcare provider, therapist, or trusted friend to ensure that you have sufficient support as you move bravely through the discomfort of unstressing to a more stable place.

INFERTILITY

Attention, new meditators! If you're not looking to get pregnant, you need to wrap it up! This is the warning I issue at the start of all my Ziva courses. Of course, if you *do* want to get pregnant, then you may be in luck: Meditation seems to have a positive impact on fertility. In fact, we have more than seventy "Ziva babies" and counting!

There are several things that likely account for this. First, there is the matter of unstressing. As any woman who has ever struggled to get pregnant has heard ad nauseam, "Just relax! Forget about trying and just have fun." Of course, that's miserable advice for someone who desperately wants a baby and *can't* simply erase the fear or the ever-present ticking clock from her brain. For every would-be grandparent or meddling aunt, however, there is good news: The science does seem to support the "just relax" plan. When the human body is in survival mode, it's focused only on self-preservation, not on perpetuating the species. Just as the immune system is put on the back burner until the immediate threat passes, fertility, too, becomes less of a priority. If the body is not sure it will be able to survive the famine/winter/tiger attack, it's not as likely to make itself optimally suited for all the beautiful work that goes into physically growing an entirely new human.

Second, a body with an acidic pH will kill off sperm much more quickly than a body with a more alkaline pH, lessening the number of possible candidates to fertilize the egg. The higher the living sperm count, the better the odds of a successful meeting between the two necessary elements.

(And if you do get pregnant, don't forget to add as many extra meditations as you want. Flooding your baby with bliss chemicals should be as much a part of your daily routine as exercising, taking prenatal vitamins and fish oil, and eliminating alcohol from your diet.)

IRRITABLE BOWEL SYNDROME (IBS)

This was quite a surprise to me, but student after student has reported a decrease in their IBS symptoms within just a few weeks of beginning Ziva. It seems to make sense, however, when you consider that one of the body's physical responses to a high-demand situation is to flood your digestive system with acid and evacuate your bowels in order to make you lighter on your feet in order to flee. If the body is allowed to recover from being in a perpetual state of fight or flight, it will no longer feel compelled to flood the stomach with acid or evacuate the bowels in the same panicked way, and the muscles of the lower digestive tract will be able to retrain themselves to function in a more regular manner.

MIGRAINES

A recent study at Wake Forest found that migraine sufferers who adopted a regular mindfulness practice reduced the duration of each headache by an average of three hours compared to a control group. I see this again and again with our in-person and zivaONLINE students—especially if the migraines are induced or exacerbated by stress. My assumption is that it has something to do with the thickening of the corpus callosum and the increased communication between the hemispheres of the brain. Ziva alumni report a decrease of migraine frequency and intensity of, on average, about 85 percent.

PARKINSON'S DISEASE

I hesitated before adding this to the list because it was just one student and it was such an unexpected response, but what I witnessed was dramatic and moving enough to make a lasting impression on me.

I had two clients, husband and wife, who booked a private course; the man was in his late sixties and had very pronounced tremors stemming from Parkinson's. On the first day of the course, I gave him his mantra; when he repeated it back to me as instructed, his tremors actually grew more intense, but as soon as he closed his eyes and began to use it silently in his mind, his tremors went away for the entirety of the meditation session and stayed away for five minutes following. Afterward, when we both opened our eyes, he asked me if I had noticed that his tremors had stopped. Not only had I noticed, I found it to be one of the most powerful and moving moments of my career. To see someone experience such an immediate change and profound relief felt like a miracle. It even brought tears to my eyes, which I tried to wipe away before he saw them so as not to make him self-conscious. The next day, he and his wife noticed that the tremors abated for roughly ten minutes after meditation, and the following day for fifteen. This continued until he was enjoying several tremor-free hours each day following his sitting. Synthetic dopamine and serotonin are often used to help calm tremors associated with Parkinson's disease, so it doesn't seem at all unlikely that their organic counterparts would have the same (or even better!) effect.

Please don't mishear me: I cannot and do not claim that meditation can cure Parkinson's disease. But I do believe that some sufferers can experience a reprieve.

PAIN

In 2015, a team of neuroscientists at Wake Forest conducted an experiment in which they evaluated people's perception of pain. Researchers tested this perception by placing a thermal probe heated to 120.2°F on the leg of each participant. The participants' pain level and emotional state were evaluated to establish a baseline, then each group was given a different form of treatment, either a placebo analgesic cream, audiobooks, "sham meditation" (that is, the instruction to just sit in a chair and breathe), or actual mindfulness training. The scientists found that the mindfulness group experienced a 27 percent reduction in physical pain perception and a 44 percent reduction in their emotional reaction to the pain, including their anxiety about the unpleasant sensation—this was dramatically higher than in the placebo groups, which showed a reduction of only 11 percent in physical perception and a 13 percent decrease in emotional response to that pain on average.[2]

Fear on top of pain can exacerbate the physical intensity of the pain. (This is the basis for most childbirth classes.) Given the opioid epidemic in the United States today, any possible alternative treatment to highly addictive medications should be explored and encouraged. Meditation offers just that. For a guided meditation for pain management, please visit www.zivameditation.com/bookbonus.

I've chosen my words carefully because I don't want anyone to think for a moment that I'm making outrageous and unsubstantiated claims. I do believe that meditation can help with a whole host of health issues, in terms of both prevention and healing. In some cases, the science is overwhelmingly in favor of a daily meditation practice. In other cases, I am at a loss to explain it, but I can't deny results I have personally experienced or witnessed with my own eyes, nor the multitude of students all sharing the same experiences. Science is catching up to what meditation practitioners have known for thousands of years. Whatever the case, fewer sick days and less pain translates into more time to get out in the world and make big things happen!

What it comes down to is this: Meditation helps you accept where you are and the possibility of healing. It has been proven to help manage pain, since the bliss chemicals it releases are a natural means of dulling unpleasant sensations. But I believe it has less to do with chemicals and more to do with how mindfulness closes the feedback loop between the brain and body. When you listen to what the body is trying to communicate, you afford it the luxury of not having to yell. Every pain is trying to communicate something to you; if you listen when it whispers, it might not have to scream. That is not to say that meditation is a placebo—quite the contrary: By allowing the mind to destress, it helps the brain do its primary job of healing and protecting the body.

Remember, your body is on your team—it wants to perform to its maximum potential. Again, I don't believe that Nature intended for us to be sick, tired, and stressed all the time. When you give your body *all* the tools it needs to succeed—including mindfulness, meditation, and manifesting—it will return the favor by allowing you to enjoy better rest and a stronger immune system, which leads to a healthier, better-performing you.

Eyes-Open Exercise

Cooling Breath

Use this exercise the next time you're on the verge of losing your cool (read: temper tantrum) or feel like you have too much acid in your belly.

Roll your tongue like a straw, then breathe in for a count of 5 and out for a count of 5, letting both the inhale and the exhale flow through your tongue straw. Allow the sensation of the air moving over your tongue to create a cooling sensation in the body and the belly.

This is a simple but effective way to calm down the next time you feel like you might lose your temper with your kids, a coworker, a customer service rep, or the driver next to you in rush-hour traffic.

Eyes-Closed Exercise

Healing Affirmations

When you're coming down with or already have an illness, use these healing affirmations as you drift off to sleep. You could record your own voice saying them, or if you prefer to have me guiding you through, visit www.ziva meditation.com/bookbonus. This link will also give you access to my very favorite guided visualization for healing.

My body knows exactly how to heal itself.

My cells are strong.

This sickness is cleaning house so that I can be even stronger.

Thank you, body. Thank you, Nature, for the lessons this is teaching me.

I'm open to receiving and incorporating these lessons.

I deserve this time to rest.

I deserve this time to heal.

I give myself permission to surrender completely to this experience because I know it's temporary.

I allow myself to experience any discomfort fully because I know the more I surrender to it, the faster I move through to the other side.

I'm already becoming stronger than I was before.

My body knows how to heal itself perfectly and quickly.

My healing is already in progress.

My healing is already in progress.

My healing is already in progress.

Ziva Case Study 4

Experiencing Cancer, Not Fighting It

CATHI PETERSON, FINANCIAL TECH FIRM MANAGER

People think that cancer has changed me. I think they're wrong.

No one knew I had just been diagnosed with breast cancer when I found myself sitting numbly at dinner with friends and couldn't help but notice something different about the couple sitting across from me. I jokingly asked if they were medicating. "No," they said, laughing, "we're *meditating*." Knowing what I was about to undertake, I simply said, "I'm gonna need some of that." That is how I found myself at Emily's door.

So for me, it all started around the same time: surgery, treatment, chemo, radiation, and meditation. Having never experienced any of those things, I didn't know what to expect. The first time I really noticed something was physically different after meditating was in the recovery room after surgery. I had just had a port put in to make for easier access to and less wear and tear on my veins during my infusions. As I lay in the recovery room, I listened to the nurses tell my sister that I couldn't go home until I could eat some food and walk around and my vitals went back to normal. The nurse told my sister she would have a few hours to kill. I heard that, propped myself up, and did my Ziva Technique. Within the hour, to everyone's surprise, I was good to go. Even the nursing staff was impressed! They said they had never seen someone's vitals come back so quickly.

In addition to my body reacting to my new meditation practice, I found myself having a profound shift in my attitude, not only to the cancer but also to the treatments themselves, which can be quite harrowing. To say it in the simplest of terms: I surrendered to the treatments instead of fighting them. Surrender doesn't mean giving up. Far from it. That simple act of surrender replaced the suffering with a sense of calm and well-being. I had the power within me to create what this experience was going to be for me.

Even my girlfriend noticed this shift and saw that I was pretty much living my life as normal. That was a bit concerning for her. It actually prompted her to ask my oncologist if the treatments were working, since I just seemed so *normal*.

The doctor looked at me and then at her and simply said, "She's bald. The medicine is working."

The doctor did take pause. She asked me what I was doing, and when I told her that I was meditating, she nodded and said, "Well, keep it up, because I don't see people responding to treatments this way very often."

As I write this, I'm celebrating the two-year anniversary of my last treatment. I believe without a doubt that it is the meditation that changed me, and I am grateful that I was shown this tool when I needed it the most. I believe in the benefits so much, in fact, that I brought Emily to my company and we have introduced meditation to more than seventy-five people at my workplace. How rewarding to see people in the elevator heading down to the meditation room, passing coworkers in the hallway who now carry that "secret weapon" of recharging in the afternoon. I cherish hearing their stories about sleeping better, noticing a different perspective, feeling less stressed, being more productive, and living as overall happier human beings.

THE (LEGIT) FOUNTAIN OF YOUTH

IF YOU DON'T BELIEVE THAT LIVING IN A STATE OF PERPETUAL stress ages a person expeditiously, just compare photos of any president on the day they took office with the day they left office. After four or more years of carrying the weight of the world on their shoulders, they invariably look older, grayer, more stooped, and more lined. The constant demands, the sleepless nights, the unending responsibilities—it all adds up to a perfect storm of rapidly accumulating stress and a rapidly aging body.

The effects of stress may be accelerated for the president, but they are just as real in our own lives. We see accumulated stress on our faces in real time, from the bags under our eyes from lack of sleep to the worry lines on our foreheads from a constantly furrowed brow. We feel it accumulating in our bodies over the gradual, creeping consequences of weeks of sleepless nights and through years of unresolved anger or sadness or both. Whatever the demands etching themselves across your face, they can lead to unrelenting pressure that intensifies with age—and our bodies pay the price. Our prematurely graying hair, our sallow skin, our aching joints, our general weariness—they all bear witness to the stress we have allowed to live rent-free in our brains and bodies. Who has ever caught a glimpse of themselves in the mirror at the end of an exhausting, emotionally draining day and thought, *I look positively radiant! I should go take my driver's license picture and new headshots right now!* Stress is not a good look on anyone.

How, exactly, does stress wreak such havoc on the body? One major factor is the same culprit we have come back to several times already: increased acid. If we revisit our tiger-attack scenario, when your brain kicks into fight-or-flight mode, it begins pumping out high doses of cortisol and adrenaline; these chemicals are (say it with me now) acidic in nature. And remember that whole thing about acid seeping into your skin so you'd taste bad if a predator tried to bite you? Yup. That contributes to an acceleration of body age, and decreases skin elasticity, too. When we live our day-to-day lives in a state of perpetual stress, we are flooding our bodies with acid. To put it rather inelegantly, we are, in essence, pickling ourselves.

» Chasing Youth

It's no secret that we live in a youth-obsessed culture. It seems that nearly every commercial for personal care products—cosmetics, lotion, grooming supplies, and so on—uses the promise of looking younger as a selling point. The cover of every women's magazine teases secrets for decreasing wrinkles or "getting that youthful glow." Every men's magazine boasts about how to "regain the strength and performance you had in your twenties!" They're all selling the dream that you can hide your age and be young again.

Our society has an unabashedly negative view on growing old, but far too often we fail to recognize the beauty of age: the wisdom that comes with time and experience; the dignity that results from loving and being at peace with your own body because of what it has borne you through; the attractiveness of maturity and confidence;

the self-assuredness that comes from reaching a point where you'll no longer tolerate anyone's bullshit. These are qualities to be celebrated, vaunted, honored. These are not the aspects of aging *anyone* should want to combat. **Too often, we're chasing youth when we should be chasing health.**

There's nothing wrong with growing older. Let me repeat that: *There's nothing in the world wrong with growing older.* It is natural and beautiful. Instead of chasing a carrot we can never capture (youth), what if we shifted our focus to chasing the things we are *actually* coveting: the glow of healthy skin, the vibrancy that accompanies a healthy diet, and the confidence and peace that are earned through daily meditation? What you'll find happens with a regular practice like the Z Technique is that *you start to become the best version of your age* **right now**. Your body will have a chance to undo physical damage, and your mind will come to a place of acceptance and celebration of what your life has been up to this point.

Our bodies are a collection of every experience, every joy, every sorrow, every meal we have eaten, every rest we have (or haven't) taken, every injury, every illness, every good decision and every bad one. Our bodies and our minds are the sum of everything we've ever been and done. This is what makes us who we are. Would you rather be someone trying to hide their age because they're ashamed of how prematurely haggard they look, or someone who can brag about their age because of how fabulous they look?

I know the difference firsthand. When you're an actress, there's a constant awareness of the age ceiling looming over your career, putting undue pressure on the rate of your success. Most actresses hide or lie about their age to make people think they're younger than they are. Now, as a meditation teacher, one of the main benefits of the thing I am selling is a reversal in body age, and I am proud of my age and how I wear it!

As the expression goes, age is only a number; it's simply an external signifier that designates the number of times our body has circled the sun—a marker of maturity and physical wear. The problem is that many of us have a flawed perspective on where that marker *should* be at each stage. We've all seen that person at our class reunion who looks like they've discovered the fountain of youth—or has, at the very least, made a deal with a fairy-tale witch for some magic beans guaranteed to eliminate wrinkles. We've also seen that person who looks like time somehow sped up in their world, aging them at a much faster rate than everyone else. Personally, I know which one I'd rather be, and I imagine you feel the same way.

Meditation helps your body repair injuries and illnesses that have stuck around due to stress's long-term effects on the body, in the form of lost or disrupted sleep, systemic inflammation, a state of chronic acidity, a decrease in mental alacrity, and pain. These are the disruptions to your body's natural aging process that accelerate and heighten the rate at which you look and feel older.

The Western notion of aging is often summed up as "You live half a dozen decades or so, then you get sick and die." That's the casual, general reality we've all seemed to accept as unavoidable . . . except it doesn't have to be. There are Ayurvedic practitioners—monks and long-term meditators—who live and thrive and age well, and then literally name the upcoming date of their death before going to the Ganges and simply dropping into the water at the moment they pass away. In other words, they die, but they don't necessarily accept the "get sick" part of the equation. As one guru described, "The yogi always wants to know the time and date of death ahead of time. He fixes it. Many years ahead he says, 'On this date, at this time I will leave, and he leaves . . . [l]eaving this body consciously without damaging this body, like you take off your clothes and walk away, you take off your body and walk away."[1] I'm not saying this needs to be your reality, but my point is that a rapid deterioration of the body and prolonged suffering before death may not be as inevitable as we tend to think.

» But Really—Meditation?

Doctors have long known that prolonged exposure to cortisol, our old stress-induced nemesis, can lead to an accumulation of visceral fat in the abdomen. Stress can literally make you gain weight in some of the most unflattering places, the effects of which are only magnified with age.[2] But the physical ripple effect of meditation goes far beyond your appearance.

In 2000, Massachusetts General Hospital partnered with Harvard Medical School to use MRIs to investigate brain mass—specifically, the specialized cortical areas of the brain that control things like cognition, which tend to thin with age, beginning around thirty. The study found that the average thickness for meditators between the ages of forty and fifty was comparable to the thickness of the average brain of people between the ages of twenty and thirty. In other words, *a regular meditation practice showed evidence of keeping the brain* up to twenty years younger *than brains without one*.[3]

Four years later, Elissa Epel, a professor of psychiatry at the University of California, San Francisco, released a study in which her team discovered that mental stress has a direct correlation on the rate at which telomeres shorten.[4] Telomeres, which are basically the caps that protect the ends of DNA strands (almost like the plastic ends that keep a shoelace from unraveling), shorten with age. Epel's study looked specifically at the telomeres on leukocytes, part of the body's immune system. Shorter leukocyte telomeres are linked to a host of age-related health concerns, including osteoporosis, Alzheimer's, and cardiovascular disease. The shorter a person's telomeres, the more vulnerable his or her cells are to degeneration and disease.

Epel's study found that among women of comparable age and physical health, telomeres were markedly shorter in women living in an environment of higher stress—the test group consisted of mothers of chronically ill children. The subjects exposed to chronic high-demand situations had notably shorter telomeres—displaying up to an additional decade's worth of decay—than the control group. In other words, researchers were able to confirm with hard science what we all already knew from experience: Stress can cause premature aging.

Epel and her team then set out to see if the effects of stress could be mitigated through natural means—namely, meditation. In a study released in 2009, they announced that meditation did, indeed, have a measurable effect on slowing the rate of deterioration of telomeres.[5]

A 2013 study by Elizabeth Hoge, M.D., a professor in the psychiatry department at Harvard Medical School, explored something similar, examining the differences in telomere lengths between meditators and nonmeditators.[6] Dr. Hoge's team discovered that not only did meditators have substantially longer telomeres than nonmeditators, there was also a correlation between telomere length and the length of time a person has been practicing meditation. Simply put, the longer a person had been meditating, the longer their telomeres were compared to those of nonmeditators.

A 2014 study by UCLA neurologist Eileen Luders found that white matter volume, which is responsible for transmitting electrical signals throughout the brain, was substantially higher for meditators than nonmeditators in seventeen of twenty different neural pathways. That means meditation had a direct correlation to the health of 85 percent of the neural pathways examined![7]

What these studies and the science that continues to emerge on an almost-daily basis seem to indicate is that meditation has a verifiably and undeniably positive effect on cellular aging.

Take a moment and consider what this means for your mental acuteness, both now and in the future. Meditation not only sets you up for present success by allowing you to bulk up your right brain, which brings the rewards of heightened intuition and awareness of the moment, but also increases your neuroplasticity, which is the brain's ability to change itself. This allows you to retain the benefits you've been working to develop. Meditation is an investment that will pay dividends in your performance capabilities for the rest of your life.

» What Kind of Body Do You Want?

Stress does age the body expeditiously, but meditation isn't magic; it's a means of purging the body of its backlog of stress. This allows the body to reset its baseline for how it physically responds to demands. Therefore, it stands to reason (and hard science backs this up, as we have just seen) that meditation is a highly effective means of helping to slow down—or even reverse—the aging process.

Within thirty seconds of the fight-or-flight response being triggered, adrenaline and cortisol are detectable in the blood; within ten minutes, those same acidic stress chemicals are present in the bone marrow. Fascinatingly, the opposite occurs with meditation: Within thirty seconds of simply sitting down with the intention to meditate, dopamine and serotonin are present in the bloodstream; after ten minutes of meditation using a technique designed for you, those same alkaline bliss chemicals are present in the bone marrow. Those chemicals have a real and lasting impact not only on your emotional state but also on the physical makeup of your body on a cellular level.

What are you creating with your actions every day: a body of fear or a body of bliss?

It's okay if your road to meditation is marked by a little bit of vanity—mine certainly was. Maybe you want to combat those crow's feet or even a bit of a paunch. But I would urge you to consider focusing on how to be the best version of your age right now, even as you seek to lengthen those telomeres. As your body begins to heal itself from stress, you'll likely begin to feel more energetic and less achy. Take advantage of that! I encourage you to get active—start jogging or doing yoga; be more conscious and deliberate about what you eat. Let meditation be just one in a series of positive choices and changes you make in your life to enable you to age gracefully. This is a second chance to treat yourself better; don't waste it.

Even if you're the type of person who has a hard time committing to healthy habits, even if you've never made a regular practice of going to the gym or cutting out gluten or going to bed early—I urge you to be open to the possibility that this may all change once you adopt this one foundational habit. I hear from my students all the time how meditation was actually the first healthy habit they were able to adopt, and how it opened the door for myriad other positive lifestyle changes. It might be as simple as a smoothie every day instead of a coffee, or a weekly yoga class, or reading in bed instead of scrolling through social media. But keep an eye out for what habits fall away innocently and spontaneously after you commit to your daily Z Technique time.

A key aspect of who you are as a high achiever is your mental acuity. As you grow older, don't you want to be able to maintain the neural pathways you've already created and continue to create more as a means of leveraging your experience into new innovations in your field? Just imagine what the cumulative results of a healthier, stronger body and mind can have on the path of a career or a life over five, ten, twenty, or even fifty years. How much more could you accomplish over the next few decades if you choose today to begin a practice that will increase your productivity and improve your performance?

As the old saying goes, "You will never be younger than you are today." The means to combat age-related deterioration is within your grasp; it's just up to you to use it.

Ziva Case Study 5

Aging Backward

HANNAH MARONEY, SALES AND MARKETING MANAGER

A few years ago, my husband and I spent a year and a half trying to get pregnant with our second child. We were in the midst of packing our life up to move from New York City to Los Angeles when I learned that one of my tubes was blocked and the other was partially blocked. Heartbreak washed over us. After relocating to L.A., we decided to connect with a fertility doctor. I took tests to assess my hormone levels, egg quality, egg production, follicle count, and so on. Across the board, my results were poor and discouraging. Because of the blocked tube, IVF became our only option. But because of the inadequate levels indicated by my blood test and my age (at the time I was thirty-eight), the doctor explained that even a successful IVF procedure would be unlikely to lead to pregnancy. We took his advice, decided not to pursue IVF, and tried to move on with our lives.

Six months later, in January 2014, I took the Ziva Meditation course, and I've been practicing meditation every day since. Early in 2015, I realized that I still wanted to have another child. I planned to revisit the fertility doctor, fully prepared for the possibility that he would deliver the same bad news (or worse, now that I was two years older) about my stats. Best case, we would be able to conceive. Worst case, I hoped that this would help close the chapter on my desire to be a mother again and enable me to move on.

I took another blood test, and my husband and I went in for another consultation. The doctor looked at my new results. Then he compared them to the results from almost two years ago. He was dumbfounded—everything had turned around for the better. He asked, "What have you changed in your life? Whatever it is, we need to bottle it! I have only seen this dramatic change once in eighteen years." I told him, "I've been meditating every day for the past two years."

Here are the results from each blood test, to show you the dramatic differences:

Test	2013	2015
Estradiol (under 80 is ideal)	313.3	39.0
Inhibin B (egg quality)	59 (avg)	94 (very good)
Anti-Mullerian hormone	.49	1.08 (above 1 is needed for IVF)
Follicle count	6 open	11 open (10 needed for IVF)

Meditation changed my body and my life. I was able to build my family a new life that is even more beautiful than I could have imagined and far surpasses the life

I had in New York, which I'd felt would be impossible to rebuild. I've made good friends and found a job that surpasses my "ideal" job in New York. I now love Los Angeles and love our neighborhood. I've run three half marathons since 2013 and have been playing my music more than ever. All these things have come to fruition because of meditating.

Two years ago, I had tremendous stress in my body (from years and years of a high-demand life, as well as moving). While I did not conceive again, meditation has helped release this stress and helped me to accept things as they are—I feel that every day. I now have scientific proof that my body changed, too, as a result, and for that I am eternally grateful.

THE "I'LL BE HAPPY WHEN . . ." SYNDROME

HOW MANY TIMES HAVE YOU SAID THE FOLLOWING WORDS: "I'll be happy when . . ."?

We all do it—sometimes in small, seemingly insignificant ways, sometimes in giant, life-altering ways. *I'll be happy when . . .*

I eat something.

I buy those shoes.

I have her wardrobe.

I hire another employee.

I close this deal.

I get that relationship.

I have that body.

I have a baby.

I make more money.

I quit this job.

I call this "I'll be happy when . . ." syndrome, and it's hard to avoid. If you're living on planet Earth, there are hundreds of thousands of people spending hundreds of billions of dollars to make you feel like your life is incomplete right now—but you *will* be happy when you get _____. The problem is that whatever appears in that blank for you will quickly be replaced by something else the moment you actually get the thing you wanted. We live in a culture that mistakenly believes it's possible to acquire our way to happiness.

» The Epidemic

Most of us have no idea we've been infected with "I'll be happy when . . ." syndrome, even though the symptoms are clear:

1. You're willing to endure misery now because you believe things will get better soon.
2. You're rigidly attached to life playing out in a particular way.
3. You find yourself in expectation more often than appreciation, with a "What have you done for me lately?" approach to life.

This syndrome can be a drain on your mental and physical energies because it makes you willing to *suffer through* your current situation, hoping and slaving away to create a better future for yourself, rather than *thriving* in it. It robs you of the opportunity to experience your bliss right here and right now.

Sometimes we confuse devotion with a right to suffer. Devotion and dedication to a cause are wonderful things; making ourselves miserable in the hope that something will shake out in our favor someday is not. The standard mind-set in society today is to live eyeball-deep in the acquisitive approach to fulfillment, where happiness hinges on the other side of what lies ahead: *I'll be happy when . . .*

I'm rich and famous.

I get married.

I have kids.

I have a million dollars.

We're willing to allow—or even encourage—ourselves to suffer in the present because of the alleged payoff in the future. We make our existence on Earth about the mythological pot of gold at the end of the rainbow. But we never find the pot of gold, do we? And if we did, we'd simply want another pot.

If you pin your happiness on climbing to the top of one mountain, what will you see when you reach the top? A beautiful view, a sense of how far you've come—*and all the other peaks you haven't climbed yet.*

What about when you were young and broke, and spent much of your day hanging out, wishing you had the money to do whatever you wanted? What was your dream? To grow up, make money, and enjoy financial freedom. When you had a bike, you wanted a car. Once you got a car, you wanted a boyfriend or girlfriend to drive around in it. Then you had that boyfriend or girlfriend and you wanted to get married. Then you got married and you wanted kids. Now you're an adult, and you miss the days when you could spend much of your day hanging out instead of working to cover your bills, saving for retirement, and managing your money all day. Our happiness becomes a carrot we keep chasing, and then we die.

The point is not to throw out your ambition, but simply to be wary of allowing your ambition to control your fulfillment and believing that you have to be unhappy now in order to be happy someday. The reality is that there is no need to make yourself miserable pursuing a dream. Happiness is only ever found in the present moment. The question is, do you have a tool to help you access it right here, right now, or are you telling yourself, *I'll be happy when . . .*

> I buy a house.
> I find my dream partner
> I get a new car.
> I get that promotion.

I'll say it again for dramatic effect, *your happiness exists in one time*—right now—*and in one place*—inside you.

This is a nice intellectual concept, but it can be frustrating if you don't have the tools to access it or experience this physically in the now. If you don't have the capability to access your immediate, internal bliss, it's not going to magically happen when you have a certain number of zeros in your bank account or sell your screenplay to Steven Spielberg or make partner in your firm.

» Bliss and Happiness Are Not Synonyms

Have you ever wished your roommate would move out so you could be happy? Or that your partner would go to therapy so you could be happy? Or that your family would start meditating so you could be happy? We've all had these kinds of thoughts, but I believe you can actually take your power back from these situations—and meditation is a powerful tool to help you do so.

Instead of giving away your power to everyone else by making your happiness dependent on theirs, why not find a means by which to access your own bliss and fulfillment? This is one of the most beautiful benefits of meditation: You actually cultivate a practice to access your own fulfillment *internally* so that when you come out of your meditation, you're no longer under the illusion that your happiness lies on the other side of anyone or anything. In this way, we start to become more self-reliant instead of object-reliant for our own happiness. When we meditate, we begin to understand that ***we hold the keys to our happiness because the practice gives us a way to access our least excited state of awareness, which is where our bliss and fulfillment have been living all along***.

This might be a good time to talk a little more about the concept of "bliss." It's a word I've used quite a lot so far in this book, and it's something we all have at least a vague concept of, but I want to clarify exactly how I'm using *bliss* in this context. *Bliss* is not a synonym for *happiness;* it's not cotton candy and bubbles and lollipops. Bliss is the piece of you that knows everything is okay—it may be an infinitesimal piece of you that knows, deep down, that things are playing out exactly as they're meant—even when you're sad, even when you're lonely, it is possible to experience bliss. In Judaism, it would be similar to what is captured in the word *shalom;* in Christianity, it would be "the peace that passes all understanding."[1] Bliss is that beautiful, powerful sense of being that trusts inherently that things are exactly as they should be. As we meditate, this background of bliss gets stronger and easier to access, even during challenging times.

BLISS: The piece of you that knows that everything is okay. It's important to note that *bliss* and *happiness* are not synonyms. It's possible to experience bliss even when you're sad, angry, or jealous. Bliss is the piece of you that knows everything is playing out as it is meant.

A lot of meditators report this shift from external chasing to internal fulfillment. Once they begin a regular practice, they find themselves becoming increasingly aware that nothing—not a new job or an amazing apartment or a new relationship or an old relationship—is the true source of their happiness. When you tap into the very source of fulfillment inside you, that deep stillness and connectedness has the profound ability to change your world. In case you didn't catch it the first time around, happiness exists in one place (within you) and one time (right now). There are no further conditions or restraints. And the more you meditate, the more you cultivate that internal bliss until you're proving it to yourself viscerally, physically, and tangibly. It starts to be your twenty-four-hour-a-day reality.

Not sure what I mean? Consider my favorite passage from the Vedas: *"The truth waits for eyes unclouded by longing."*

We've all been there. We've all wanted that one job to be the perfect job so badly that we forgot to read the out clause in the contract; we all wanted that one person to be our perfect person so badly that we put blinders on and overlooked the fact that on the first date they were drinking too much and didn't tip the server (just me? cool, moving on . . .); we've all wanted that extra zero in our bank account so badly that we were willing to do whatever it took to get it. The thing is, when we're racing or, worse, suffering through our lives with this longing, it makes us very attached to the outcomes of our desires. Have you ever been so attached to the outcome of something—a first date, a job interview, closing a deal—that you ended up sabotaging the opportunity just when you had your big shot because you came across as way too desperate or needy?

What happens when we meditate and de-excite the nervous system is that the mind settles, the body settles, and, for a few moments, we find ourselves spontaneously and innocently in a space of no thought, no mantra; *we move out of the realm of thinking and into the realm of being.* We access our least excited state of awareness, which is where our bliss and fulfillment hang out. That's right—our bliss and fulfillment . . . hanging out . . . right there within us the whole time, just waiting to be accessed. Every spiritual text has been saying this since the beginning of time: What you seek is in you. We even have this saying painted on a giant mural in our New York City studio. It's great as an intellectual concept, but it's much more powerful to be able to experience that twice a day every day—which is exactly what this practice provides. It gives you a means by which to experience contentment internally.

When you experience that inner bliss and fulfillment, it wipes the longing away from your lens of perception because the mind and body cannot fathom anything that would bring them greater fulfillment than what they are already experiencing in the meditation. As a result, the mind falls silent. And when you come out of the meditation, you've wiped some of the longing away from your lens of perception because you just accessed your fulfillment internally. The result is that life comes into sharper focus—you are no longer under the illusion that your happiness will come on the other side of any person, place, or thing.

This, in turn, allows you to see things more accurately for what they really are, which means you're less likely to make a mistake. And what is a mistake? *It is a miss-take: You took something to be one thing when it was actually something else.* All too often, it's our own desperate desire to find that elusive sense of fulfillment in something external that leads us to view it with "eyes clouded by longing." When we remove those clouds, we can see the truth more plainly— the truth about people, the truth about our circumstances, and the truth about our desires. The potential to recognize your bliss—the bliss that your own body is capable of creating and fostering—is something you carry with you at all times. Think about how amazing that is for a moment. No other human and no other thing can provide it for you; you are already entirely enough. You simply need to learn how to access that limitless source of fulfillment waiting for you inside.

» Detachment Is Sexy (Neediness Is Not)

Once you start to commit to your twice-a-day Z Technique, you will start to see for yourself that you're no longer under the illusion that your happiness exists on the other side of any person, place, thing, or achievement. As a result, you'll find yourself becoming more adaptable to the circumstances that surround you, rather than insisting that everyone else change. Because you're no longer under the illusion that you're dependent on anything external for your happiness, you're no longer emotionally devastated when those things inevitably change or "fail you." That's not to say you won't feel sadness or disappointment in certain situations, of course, but those fallible things will no longer have the power to control your mood the way they once did.

This reclaiming of your power is not some big, public proclamation where you announce to the world over social media, *"Attention, everyone:* I'm taking my power back and I don't need any of you!" Tempting as that may be at times, what I'm talking about is actually a very subtle internal shift in your perception of what is necessary for you to feel a sense of fulfillment. Suddenly, you begin to carry yourself differently and interact with society in a more confident and self-assured way, all because you've embraced the beautiful and radical notion that you are *enough*. This is a much more powerful and elegant way to live than to constantly be in pursuit of something that will never fully satiate all your longings.

Detachment is sexy; neediness is not. I love this concept so much that I want to make a T-shirt that reads on the front, DETACHMENT IS SEXY, and on the back, NEEDINESS IS NOT. Rather than seeming desperate, a person who has tapped into the very source of bliss gives off an air of contentedness that projects unflappable self-confidence. And isn't that the dream, after all—to be the person in the room who is most comfortable in his or her own skin? That's what I mean by "taking your power back." Instead of being dependent on other people's decisions, judgments, and actions for your sense of happiness, you will have a healthy level of detachment with your potential romantic partners, with clients, with colleagues, with possessions, and with ambition. You don't need anyone's approval to feel good about life, nor do you need any object or status symbol to feel complete. Happiness is truly an inside job.

» Desires and Manifestation

"Hold up, Emily. In chapter 1, you spent a lot of time talking about how awesome and powerful manifesting is, but now you're telling me that the stuff I want is coming from a place of neediness and keeping me down?"

It might seem like the two are in conflict, but bear with me while I explain the difference.

When you make the decision to up-level your life by incorporating twice-a-day sitting into your routine, you're essentially embracing the most beautiful kind of surrender—trusting that Nature has your back and relinquishing control. These are two extremely difficult things for many of us to do, but when we're clinging to our desires so tightly, our hands are too clenched to receive what Nature has in store.

Can manifesting become just another addiction, if all we do is spend our meditation time thinking about all the awesome things we're wishing for? Absolutely! As we said before, manifesting is *not* magical thinking. Manifesting isn't simply an opportunity to redirect your neediness to the universe. Manifesting *is*, however, a chance for you to get crystal clear on your goals and be disciplined about taking time to imagine them as if they are happening now. As you do this, you open yourself up to what Nature may have in store for you, if you're ready to receive it. Here is where the Z Technique shines; the combination of meditation and manifesting is so much more powerful than the sum of its parts. Meditation supercharges your manifesting ability because flooding your brain and body with dopamine twice a day helps you release your death grip on your desires, so you are no longer under the illusion that your happiness lies on the other side of the attainment of them. Paradoxically, this allows you to hear those subtle whispers from Nature. It also helps to increase something I call "deserving power," which is what you believe you deserve. Reminder, we don't get what we want in life, we get what we believe we deserve.

Manifesting is not an extension of "I'll be happy when . . ." syndrome because you'll quickly come to recognize your happiness does not hinge on the desire becoming reality. When it does, of course, that's a beautiful thing. But what you'll begin to see is Nature's GPS, unfogged and calibrated for your personal journey, directing you toward the path it wants you to explore; your manifestations will begin to feel less like plans you're dreaming up on your own and more like manuals to prepare you to maximize the opportunities and experiences that lie ahead.

This leads us to the final and most important point on this topic: delivering your fulfillment to the world.

» The Best Way Out

If reading about the "I'll be happy when . . ." syndrome is hitting a little too close to home, the first thing to know is that you aren't alone. Nearly every single person in contemporary Western society has, at one time or another, struggled with it. There are billions of dollars of advertising built on top of keeping us in that mind-set. The question is whether you want to stay in that struggle or transcend it.

Remember that, according to the Vedas, your happiness exists in one place—inside you—and in one time—right now. Easier said than done, right? Well, meditation's benefits extend to this aspect of finding fulfillment as well, because it helps you recognize how you can effectively devote yourself to something bigger than you. As your longing is wiped away from your perception, you'll begin to perceive your deepest desires as rooted not in a desperate scramble for happiness, but borne out of it. In other words, *meditation allows you to transition from being a bag of* **need looking for fulfillment to fulfillment looking for need**.

I want you to think about that for a moment. Instead of being someone full of unmet wants, going through life looking for a way to get your needs met, you can be someone full of contentment, going through life looking for needs that *you can meet,* looking for ways to contribute. When you're in tune with your own fulfillment internally, you can deliver that to the people and circumstances you encounter. Soon, you'll be able to see specific needs around you more clearly and think creatively about how to meet them. Quite innocently and spontaneously, you will start to find joy in being of service.

What's more beautiful than complete and total devotion to something you believe in, something bigger than yourself? That something can be anything you consider worthwhile that extends beyond the parameters of your own life: creativity, being a parent, being a partner, devoting yourself to your divinity, helping the homeless, saving the environment, mentoring children. It doesn't matter what the thing is; what matters is that you throw your heart and soul into it. *This* is the difference between devotion and suffering. Suffering for a dream keeps the focus on you and what you get from it. Devotion removes the ego—it gets the self out of the way *because the self is already fulfilled*.

I truly believe that the more you devote yourself to something bigger than yourself, the more you'll enjoy yourself along the way. Joy multiplies—that is, rather than focusing on making one person (yourself) happy, you'll be focusing on the collective, giving to many people, animals, or the Earth. Who cares if there's a pot of gold at the end of an imaginary rainbow if you're unhappy chasing after it your entire life? Who cares if the destination is amazing if the journey there was terrible? Life is short—why embrace unnecessary misery? But giving because it feels great to give, creating for the sake of creation, becomes the reward in itself.

This is at the heart of countless religious teachings, and for good reason. When you take yourself and your individual goals out of the top spot and focus instead on the betterment of someone or something else, you become an active participant in the creation of a better world, which lifts everyone. I work with a lot of young entrepreneur clients who are inspiring to me—they're so devoted to identifying unmet needs and determining what gifts they have that can best serve those needs . . . and then *doing* it.

But how do you figure out what to make the object of your devotion? If you haven't yet found your passion, it can be frustrating to hear other people talk about their life's work or purpose. How did they find it? And why haven't you found yours? Don't we all secretly wish we'd been born with an instruction manual—a little set of directions for how to live our lives? I actually think we were, but most of us don't really know how to listen to it. The idea that we each have only one mission or one quest is debilitating and can keep us from ever getting started. I don't think you have only one mission; I think each person has a number of challenges to solve. Which challenges you solve and how you solve them—well, that's up to you.

But you don't have to figure it out alone. I have found four questions that can help you narrow down the search from a world full of possibilities to a much narrower, much more personal cause that is meaningful to you. These questions can help you learn how to trust your desires as Nature's GPS and get you out of the "I'll be happy when . . ." syndrome.

Ask yourself:

1. What is the most pressing need of the time?
2. How do my gifts best serve the need of the time?
3. Which of these gifts do I want to use?
4. Which of these gifts do I want to use right now?

So how does meditation play into this? Well, let's review what we know about meditation: It's the fastest way to release stress, which means you can make better decisions. It activates your right brain, which means your intuition gets stronger and more honed every day. When we meditate, we can more elegantly tell the difference between our addictive longings (money, sex, perceived success, and so on coming from individuality) and our intuitive desires, which are "downloaded" from totality. Plus, as you know by now, within thirty to forty seconds of starting a session, your brain and body flood with the bliss chemicals dopamine and serotonin; when you're full of bliss, you can approach your desires and decisions from a clear-eyed state of fulfillment rather than a state of neediness. Sounds nice, right?

Remember that during the practice you are going to learn in the next chapter, you're actually tapping into the source of fulfillment when your body releases the bliss chemicals it already makes naturally; as a result, you'll feel less confused by what you should do because you'll be making decisions from a place of contentment rather than suffering or panic. Because they'll be most closely aligned with your beliefs and goals, they'll also ultimately end up being the most prudent, most creative, and even the most lucrative decisions.

One of my favorite quotes is, "Water the flowers, not the weeds." It's so simple and yet so powerful. That is ultimately the goal of combining meditation and manifestation: We put our attention on what we want to grow—the meaningful, the powerful, and the blissful—and let neediness, dissatisfaction, and stress wither away. Meditation helps pluck those negative attributes out of our body and nervous system. Manifestation, meanwhile, helps us get specific about what things have the potential to blossom into something beautiful.

The thing to remember is that breaking free from "I'll be happy when . . ." syndrome does not mean your goals and ambitions will go away; just the opposite, in fact. You'll very likely experience a stronger drive to accomplish than ever before. The difference is that your attachment to the outcome will not be so paralyzing because you know your happiness is not outcome dependent. *You'll be free to think and act with a creativity and confidence that you may never have known before,* and your decision-making will be steered by sharp intuition rather than clouded by fear or desperation.

Of course, you'll still feel the full range of human emotions; meditation doesn't turn your feelings off. When you learn how to access your inner bliss, you do not negate your capacity for sadness, jealousy, nervousness, and the like. Those thoughts and doubts and nagging notions are part of the human experience, but as you grow in your daily practice, your internal bliss will grow as well, along with your ability to tap into it more easily.

Eyes-Open Exercise

Water the Flowers, Not the Weeds

Gratitude Exercise: Every morning and every night, write down three things you are grateful for. You could do this on your phone (my personal preference), so you always have your journal with you to reflect on when you need it. Oprah says this is the most important habit she ever adopted. This exercise helps train your brain to look for things that are going right instead of constantly searching for problems you think you have to solve.

Gratitude is one of the fastest ways to break yourself out of "I'll be happy when . . ." syndrome. You'll already be practicing this every day as you transition between the meditation and manifesting portions of the Z Technique (which we will discuss in chapter 8), so this exercise should get easier until it becomes second nature. Don't worry too much about getting it "right." Even on the days when you feel there is nothing going your way, simply asking the question "What am I grateful for?" is enough to change the chemistry of your brain!

» 8 «

THE Z TECHNIQUE

AT LAST—THIS IS IT! THIS IS THE WHOLE REASON YOU PICKED up this book in the first place: You're on board, you've been warned about the potential mental and physical detox, and you're ready to learn the Z Technique! Let's do this.

We'll start by breaking down the 3 M's of the Z Technique.

» The 3 M's

As a system, the Z Technique consists of three M words: Mindfulness, Meditation, and Manifesting. Each aspect contributes something important to the overall practice. And the whole is indeed greater than the sum of its parts. To recap: **Mindfulness** *helps you deal with stress in the present moment;* **meditation** *gets rid of stress from the past; and* **manifesting** *helps you create your dreams for the future.* I like to think of the three parts of the Z Technique as the appetizer, main course, and dessert.

» A Day in the Life

It's best to do your morning sitting just after waking so you start your day fully rested and at peak creativity and productivity. Get up (a bit earlier than usual), go to the bathroom, brush your teeth, and splash a little water on your face if you like. But best to do this before breakfast, coffee, or computer time. Since coffee is a stimulant, it can counteract the de-exciting effects of the meditation portion and make you feel as if you're having a panic attack. Just trust me on this one, and enjoy your coffee after you finish your morning sitting.

The one notable exception to the first-thing-upon-waking-after-going-to-the-bathroom rule is if you're a parent of a young child (or children). Y'all have different priorities, and your morning is definitely not your own in this stage of your life. I get that things are a little catch-as-catch-can for you, so simply adapt this morning routine as best you can for your schedule. If your child has a predictable sleep pattern, I would recommend setting an alarm half an hour before he or she usually wakes up so you'll have that time for yourself. It's worth it. I promise. Similarly, you may need to feed your pets before you do your sitting—all good. Simply know that the goal is to do this as close to waking as possible, because once the momentum of your day starts, it's much harder to get to the chair.

Your second sitting will occur sometime in midafternoon or early evening—not immediately after lunch, since the tryptophan in your turkey sandwich might make you sleepy—but anytime after you're done digesting lunch and before your evening meal. For most people with typical work schedules, their second meditation falls somewhere between noon and eight P.M., ideally before the afternoon slump sets in. The goal is to proactively give your brain the rest and recharging it needs to stay in top form for the *entire* day, rather than going cross-eyed staring at your computer at five P.M. or reaching for a third or fourth cup of coffee to power through your latest project. You don't have to be rigidly attached to the same schedule every day; if you normally meditate around three thirty P.M. but you have a call scheduled that day, simply bump your meditation earlier so you'll be finished before your attention is needed elsewhere. (This will also help you feel as if you have superhuman negotiating powers during the call.)

Remember that it's important not to put off your meditation until too late in the evening. Just as you wouldn't be well served by a nap at nine P.M. if you plan on going to bed at eleven, meditating too late can make sleep difficult, since your body will have just had such deep and restorative rest during meditation. If you meditate too close to bedtime, you may find yourself lying awake with tons of energy and loads of great ideas—but no one to tell them to but your cat.

When you're ready to begin the Z Technique, consider where you'll physically place yourself. Contrary to popular belief, it's not necessary to have one designated space in your home decked out with candles, incense, white string lights draped artfully from the ceiling, and Enya playing on a loop. Is that lovely? Sure. Is it relaxing? Probably. Is it necessary? Nope. One of the drums I like to beat over and over is this: *Meditation is the ultimate portable device.* Do it on the train, in a park, at your desk, in the dark—it sounds like a children's book, but the truth is that you really can meditate in any setting. Anywhere you have the ability to think a thought and a place to sit, you will now have the ability (read superpower) to meditate.

If you have the choice between bright or dim lights, a loud setting or a quiet one, go with the low-light, low-noise option if you can, simply because it will be more enjoyable. If you want to create a special space that's decorated in a calming or meaningful way, that's totally fine—it's just not necessary for this to be effective. Meditation is about internal change that extends to your external life. *Any space can become a meditative space because you bring that significance to it simply through your intention to meditate and having solid training in a technique designed for you, not for a monk.*

The only necessary thing is a place to sit with your back supported and your head free. Your legs can be crossed, stretched out, pulled up toward your chest—comfort is key. Make sure you're able to lean against something while allowing your neck to flop forward or backward as it will. (Remember all those lectures on posture your mom gave you growing up? Now's the time to toss those out the window.)

This may be confusing if you're used to seeing beautiful pictures of Himalayan yogis or lululemon-clad women sitting cross-legged on a cliff with nothing supporting their very erect spines, doing something fancy with their fingers. There's nothing wrong with this, and it certainly does make for a great photo, but that style of meditation is more monk-like. Take a moment to ask yourself, *Am I a monk?* If the answer is no, then don't stress about perfect posture or an elaborate sitting ritual. Remember, the Z Technique is all about meditating to get good at life. This is meditation for busy people with busy minds and it is designed to be integrated into your life on the go.

Now find a comfortable seat, and we'll begin with the mindfulness portion of our practice—the first of the 3 M's. Remember that mindfulness is the art of bringing your awareness into the present moment: Don't fret about what your meditation is going to be like in a few minutes or try to get your desires ready for the manifestation exercise. At Ziva, we like to use mindfulness as a runway into the meditation. It is more of a left-brain, waking-state practice, so it gives you something to do on your way into the restful surrender that is meditation.

» The First M: Mindfulness—Come to Your Senses

Begin with your eyes closed, your back supported, and your head free.

Take a moment to enjoy the easy flow of your breath in and out of your lungs, then gradually shift your attention to all the sounds happening around you. Hear what you're hearing. Listen for the most prominent sound in the room—maybe it's your coworker on the phone or the air-conditioning clicking on. Then, after a few breaths, gently shift your awareness to the subtlest sound you can detect—the sound of your own breathing or ambient noise from the hallway. Your "goal" is to attune yourself to the subtle sonic differences that surround you, gently bringing your awareness to every sound happening in the space right now.

Enjoy this for a few more breaths and then, on your next inhale, gently bring your awareness to the *most prominent* tactile sensation in your body right now—perhaps it's the feeling of your bum in the chair or a sore knee. Recognize it and then shift your attention to the *subtlest* tactile sensation, whether it's your hair lightly brushing your neck or the feeling of the air entering and exiting your lungs. Take care that you're not judging the sensations as "good" or "bad"— simply notice what is the most prevalent and most subtle.

After a few moments, shift your awareness to your sense of sight. Yes, your eyes will be closed, but what can you see? Blackness? A sliver of light coming through the space where your eyelids meet? Perhaps you even see colors in your mind's eye.

Gradually shift your attention to your sense of taste. Even though you aren't currently eating something (right?), your mouth will always have some kind of taste to it, whether it's toothpaste or coffee or peanut butter. After a few breaths, start to notice the subtlest taste— maybe you can taste the salad dressing from your lunch or the minty flavor of the gum you enjoyed afterward, or maybe it's nothing more than a sense of your mouth being acidic or dry.

Finally, let yourself smell what you're smelling. As you continue to breathe easily, notice the most prominent smell you can detect. Is it your own hairspray or cologne, or the candle you're burning? What is the subtlest smell in the room—flowers, or simply the smell of dust heating in the radiator? Perhaps you notice the absence of smell entirely.

Now I invite you to pull the lens of your awareness back and simultaneously bring all five senses into your awareness at once: Notice the loudest and softest sounds, the most prominent and gentlest touches, the light and the darkness, the taste and the hint of a taste, the strongest smell and the weakest. As you bring these all together concurrently, you are awakening your simultaneity of consciousness—your complete awareness of surroundings and self.

Let your breath be easy and natural as you start to allow yourself to include everything happening around you into this mindfulness experience. Giving yourself permission to be in the moment, the *right now.* Letting go of the old idea that noise is a "distraction" and simply including everything that is happening inside this experi-ence. Flow through all five senses a few times until you feel like you can start to hold all five in your awareness at the same time. Give yourself permission to be so deliciously human and present. Your stress hangs out in the past and the future; your bliss is always found in the now. This simple but powerful exercise will help you use your five senses as a tool to get yourself into the body and into the now. Use it to move toward your bliss, not away from your stress. This is a subtle but important distinction.

You may want to spend a few days practicing Come to Your Senses on its own. This will help you handle stress in the present moment. Then, when you're ready, you can add the meditation portion. If you're interested in having an audio of me guiding you through the mindfulness portion of the technique, you can access a video of Come to Your Senses at www.zivameditation.com/bookbonus.

After you complete the mindfulness, move on to the meditation portion, the second M of the Z Technique, in which you'll use a specific mantra to de-excite your nervous system to help you access that deep, healing rest.

» The Second M: Meditation

As you transition from the mindfulness portion to the meditation portion, you can take the sense of expanded awareness and inclusiveness with you into the surrender that is meditation. (Surrender, by the way, sometimes carries the negative connotation of "giving up," but I invite you to think of it as trusting your body, trusting this practice, and ultimately trusting that your intuition will rise to the surface so you can trust yourself even more.)

SURRENDER: Trusting that Nature has more information than you do; the act of releasing yourself to something bigger, wiser, and more powerful than you. It does not mean giving up or quitting—it means trusting that a higher power (God, Nature, the universe, whatever term you use) has your back!

The key to making the transition as seamless as possible is to not use too much force with the mantra you are about to receive. You don't say, *Okay, brain! Mantra time!* and then start chanting the mantra over and over; instead, let it live in the back of your brain effortlessly and innocently. Imagine that your mantra is that super-hot person at the bar who you know is watching you; you definitely want to engage, but you don't want to just run up and start aggressively talking a mile a minute. Be a little coy and let the mantra come to you.

Don't actually say the mantra out loud; that would be chanting, which is a different practice altogether. In fact, you don't even have to be precise about the tempo. Simply hear the mantra like a whisper of an echo in the back of your mind, more like a sound or an instrument than a word. I specifically and deliberately chose the mantra or "mind anchor" we are using, but this is not about repeating the word itself.

» The Mantra

Just what is this mysterious mantra I keep teasing you with? If you were bracing for some magical sound that will transport you into a cosmic abyss of black hole nothingness, I'm sorry to disappoint you—this word is very simple. Take comfort in the fact that it's the combination of the mantra and the effortless technique that makes this meditation so effective. When people learn with us in person at Ziva, they are given their own personalized mantra. In the online training, you are taught how to choose your own mantra from a specific curated list. I wish I could deliver the same level of guidance via a book, but I have no way of making sure you have face-to-face support or finish reading this book to fully understand the capabilities and impact of this new tool. Since the personalized mantras are so powerful, we have purposefully chosen a gentler, universal word for you to use as your mental anchor.

The word you'll use is simple and effective. You'll gently hear the word "*one*" in the background of your mind, helping to usher you into the subtler states of consciousness.

Remember what we discussed about mantras back in chapter 1—how they're sounds designed to function as "mind vehicles" to de-excite your nervous system? And remember how you promised you wouldn't make the mistake of regarding Mindfulness, Meditation, and Manifestation as "magical thinking"? Well, I'm holding you to that. *One* as your mantra is a perfect example of what I'm talking about. The word could potentially mean a dozen different things: unity; becoming number *one* in your field; the *one* thing you are prioritizing. It could absolutely signify any of those things to you. But it doesn't have to. You can simply enjoy the sound of the word, happening faintly in the background of your mind. The whole point is to allow the mind vehicle to induce this deep, healing rest while you enjoy a brief surrender—just a few minutes out of your day—and the benefits it brings. The point is not for you to ruminate on the word in an effort to uncover some deeper significance or profound insight. To do so would be attempting to steer the direction of your meditation, which either shifts you into "contemplation" or launches you out of the *nishkam karma* style of meditation entirely and into focusing. You will start to find that the word takes on a life of its own. It will get fainter and finer over time.

I can hear you now: *That seems a bit too simple. I say the word "one" at least a dozen times a day and it hasn't done any of the stress-releasing or brain-boosting things you've been talking about for the past seven chapters.* Sometimes the most profound truths are the simplest. And we never want to confuse simplicity with weakness. The power in this practice comes from the simplicity.

You're absolutely correct: The word won't induce any mental change if you're using it in your left-brain, waking state with the intention to communicate an idea. In this instance, you're using the word as an anchor and setting your body and mind up for deep rest and surrender. A car key doesn't do too much sitting on your kitchen counter, either. You have to know which car to put it in and how to turn it on.

The single most important piece of meditation advice you can hold with you as you dive in is this: Thoughts are not the enemy. Remember that the mind thinks involuntarily just like the heart beats involuntarily, so please don't try to give your mind a command to be silent. That will never work and will only lead to frustration. Instead, know that thoughts are okay—they're actually a useful part of this process and now you have your trusty anchor, *one,* to come back to when you notice you've taken a mental field trip.

Your meditation period—the part of the Z Technique that you will soon see can feel a bit like a nap sitting up—should last about fourteen minutes. Eventually you will need only about one minute of the mindfulness appetizer. So one minute of mindfulness leading into fourteen minutes of meditation equals fifteen. Set your *internal* alarm for fifteen minutes—you may be surprised how accurate your natural clock is if you give it a chance to be trained. It's no problem if you want to check your watch. I encourage it. Keep it located nearby and check as often as you like! You may even find that you tend toward a certain pattern. Personally, I find myself checking halfway through and then feel myself come out of the meditation right at my end time. I advise students who are beginning their practices to set a backup alarm for a few minutes after the allotted sitting time. That will help ease paranoia about going long and missing a whole day of meetings if you accidentally fall asleep. (In eleven years of twice-daily meditations, I've only fallen asleep twice, so it's actually far less of a concern than most people think.) This is one of the reasons it's so important to sit with your back supported but your head free; if your head is supported, you're much more likely to click over into sleep.

Ideally, however, I want you to train your own internal clock so that you can move away from relying on any kind of an alarm at all. *But why can't I set an alarm, Emily?* Simply put, they're too alarming. Instead, simply check a conveniently located timepiece. It's best to use a watch or a clock or the cable box and throw your phone in the nearest river, but if you don't own any other timepiece and *have* to use your phone, there's a free app called The Clocks that turns your phone into a giant digital clock, so you don't have to touch or swipe or enter any codes to see the time. If you're curious about how much time has passed, just check. If your fifteen minutes aren't up yet, simply close your eyes and float back to the mantra. I would rather you check your clock a hundred times than get yanked out of the meditation by your alarm going off (yes, even that gentle *om* from your meditation timer app). And the reason for that is something I call "the meditation bends."

THE MEDITATION BENDS: Headaches, eye strain, and irritability caused by coming up and out of your meditation too quickly.

In scuba diving, if you surface too quickly, the gas bubbles trapped in your body's tissues will expand, causing the bends, a painful and even dangerous physical sensation in which your joints cramp closed. In meditation, if you pull yourself out too quickly, you'll likely deal with headaches, eye strain, and irritability. The brain and optic nerves don't have pain receptors, so they can't tell you they are hurting the instant you jolt out of meditation, but a sudden transition from resting to waking state can be too shocking. Instead, we want to allow the brain and optic nerve to gently readjust to a waking state. *No alarms* except for your backup, don't-sleep-through-the-day-while-you're-learning-to-meditate insurance policy. If you come out of your meditation too quickly and it causes irritability and headaches about thirty minutes later, then you've just wasted your time; you can have headaches and irritability without meditating twice a day.

The way to avoid the meditation bends is to add a two-minute "safety stop" at the end of your meditation, in which you cut the cord to the anchor of your mantra and allow yourself to float back upward to a waking state while keeping your eyes closed. This allows your eyes and brain to gradually readjust. And it's during this two-minute period that you incorporate your practice of manifesting.

» The Third M: Manifesting

We start the manifesting portion from a place of gratitude. This doesn't have to take a long time. Simply ask yourself the question *What am I grateful for right now?* Practice gratitude for the relationships in your life, for your home and health, for your family and for opportunities, for the beautiful sunset last night, or for making your bus by the skin of your teeth this morning. Whatever is on your heart that makes you feel thankful, acknowledge it. ***Nature/God/higher power—whatever you call it—likes to be paid attention to, just like the rest of us.*** You know how we all have that one friend who never seems grateful for anything—they just ask and ask and ask, and you eventually stop doing favors for that person because they don't seem to care enough to give you a shout-out or offer help in return? Don't be that person. Recognize the beautiful gifts in your life, no matter how insignificant or clichéd or esoteric or shallow they might seem. There is no wrong way to show thankfulness for your blessings except not to acknowledge them at all. This may seem simple (are you noticing a pattern of simple-but-powerful tools here?), but there is some fascinating neuroscience research coming out about gratitude. Scientists are finding that even on the days when you don't feel like you have anything to be thankful for, just asking the question "What am I grateful for?" is enough to change the chemistry of your brain.[1] This simple practice trains you to look for everything that is going right in your life so you can start to more effectively water the flowers and not the weeds.

The more you stimulate these neural pathways through practicing gratitude, the stronger and more automatic they become. On a scientific level, this is an example of Hebb's Law, which states, "neurons that fire together wire together." But it's also something you can see plainly in everyday life: If you're forging a new path through the woods, the first trip is the most challenging, and you have to be deliberate. But the more times the path is traveled, the more defined it becomes and the easier it is to follow. Your brain works the same way: The more times a certain neural pathway is activated (neurons firing together), the less effort it takes to stimulate the pathway the next time (neurons wiring together).

The gratitude is setting you up for the third M of the Z Technique: manifesting. Every gold-medal athlete, every Oscar or Tony winner, every successful CEO has first created a mental blueprint of how they will go about pursuing their goals and what it will *feel* like when they accomplish them. After you finish your fifteen minutes of mindfulness and meditation, you will check your timepiece, let go of the mantra anchor, and move into the safety stop. The safety stop only takes two minutes. You begin with a moment of gratitude, then I invite you to think of **one dream, one goal, or one desire** and imagine it as if it were your **current reality**. This is really the trick to manifesting: Imagine the dream as if it is happening *now*. Don't picture it as something that will happen down the road; give yourself permission to see, feel, hear, taste, and smell every aspect of that desire as if it were happening to you *right now* in your current, immediate reality. Explore it in your mind like you're a little kid playing pretend. Claim it as yours. As you take the time to marinate in this dream, allowing your imagination to color in the details all around you, pay particular attention to how this feels. We all think we are chasing a goal, but the reality is, we're chasing how we assume the goal will make us *feel*. This exercise gives us the gift of experiencing the joy, the accomplishment, the generosity in the now.

Once you can feel and see this dream happening all around you, ask yourself who would be the first person you call to share the news with. Imagine that conversation. What would you say? Are you crying? Laughing? Now imagine their response. Are they laughing? Crying? Squealing with delight? Take a moment to receive their enthusiasm and let that fuel your dream.

And then, when you're ready, slowly open your eyes and come back to your surroundings. Congratulations! You, my friend, have just completed your very first Z Technique!

» Make the Z Technique Nonnegotiable

This version of meditation may be different from every version you've ever heard of before. I am suggesting you don't have to clear your mind, that it's okay to notice and even include all the sounds and sensory experiences happening around you; there is no focusing. And on top of all that, you don't need to set an alarm or use a meditation app to time your sitting. If this all seems too far from the disciplined, focused attempts at clearing your mind you've used before, ask the question *How's that going for me? Am I noticing a significant return on my time invested? Have I been committing to a daily practice?* If you're ready to try something different, here's the recap of what we have learned so far:

Sit with your back supported, head free.

Have a timepiece near you (set your *internal* alarm for 15 minutes).

Begin mindfulness—Come to Your Senses: 1 to 2 minutes.

Gently let your new mantra float to you: 13 to 14 minutes.

Let go of the mantra but keep your eyes closed for a "safety stop": 2 minutes.

Practice manifesting: During the 2-minute safety stop, imagine a dream as if it is happening now.

Open your eyes and deliver your greatness to the world.

Please review this chapter as often as you need to, until the process of transitioning from one phase of the Z Technique to the next becomes second nature; I would hate for you to pull yourself out of a delicious meditation just to rifle through these pages trying to remind yourself of what the next step is. Even if you do, however, be gentle with yourself and remember that even a "bad" meditation is better than no meditation at all. ***Don't let perfect be the enemy of good, and don't let good be the enemy of done.*** If you forget what to do next or find yourself swinging your mantra around your brain like a baseball bat or forget to put your phone on silent and your grandma calls to say hello smack-dab in the middle of your session—no sweat. You didn't just derail the entire course of your meditation career. You are making progress, and you will continue to do so each time you get in the chair. If you want extra support, you can always listen to me guiding you through certain portions of this practice at www.zivameditation.com/bookbonus. Remember that a meditation practice is just that—a practice. There is no perfection.

» A Word of Warning

Before we move on, it's important that I address something that is asked in every class I teach: "Can I use this style of meditation to calm myself if I am in a 'stressful' situation, like being stuck in traffic?" The answer is a resounding no—at least for the meditation portion. You can safely use the Come to Your Senses portion with your eyes open. There are several calming mindfulness exercises on the Ziva website (zivameditation.com) that can be great to employ in those types of situations. However, given that you will want to stay fully awake, alert, and wholly cognizant of your surroundings when you're operating a motor vehicle, supervising small children, or standing in front of a roomful of people, you definitely do *not* want to send yourself into that fourth state of consciousness.

The point of the Z Technique is to help you prime your brain and nervous system in such a way that you're better prepared to respond to these types of situations in a healthy and productive way, not to bring you immediate calm in the moment. What the Z Technique does is actually help get to the root of the problem, treating the cause rather than the symptom.

» The Five Things That Happen Most Commonly in a Sitting

It would be ludicrous to try to give your heart a command to stop beating or your nails a command to stop growing. Your body simply doesn't work that way, and yet people have this notion that an "ideal" meditation is one in which they are able to turn their minds off. I've been meditating for more than eleven years, and I've never once had a thought-free meditation. Not one time. So either I have no business teaching this, or else a completely quiet mind is not the point. You can decide for yourself after you finish this book and have a few weeks of practice under your belt; in the meantime, please be gentle with yourself, but even beyond being gentle, allow yourself to be curious. I challenge you to let go of all your preconceived notions of what meditation *should* be and simply use this tool and see how you feel. This is actually why I titled this book *Stress Less, Accomplish More*—it's ultimately about the end result. If you're allergic to the word *meditation*, great. Just try the Z Technique and see how you feel. I cannot say this enough—if you've tried meditation and felt like you were failing because you couldn't "clear your mind," *that is not a problem with this kind of practice*. Give yourself the gift of a beginner's mind. Beginners learn more than experts eight days a week.

Thinking during meditation is actually an indicator that some stress is leaving the body. This is where the healing happens. Better out than in, right? When you feel those thoughts coming up and out, know that it is stress exiting your nervous system.

If you remember just one thing from this whole book, let it be this: A deep meditation is no better for you than a shallow meditation. I'm going to say that again for dramatic effect. *A deep meditation is no better for you than a shallow meditation.* I am defining a deep meditation as one in which the time passes quickly, you have few thoughts, and you generally enjoy the sitting. In a shallow meditation, the time may pass more slowly, you may feel like you are just sitting there having thoughts the whole time, and you may not enjoy the sitting itself. Both are beneficial for you. A deep meditation means the body is getting deep rest; a shallow meditation means the body is releasing stresses in the form of thoughts. One is not better for you than the other. Write it on your mirror, make a T-shirt, tattoo it on your forehead. I know it sounds crazy and counter to everything you have likely heard about meditation so far, but it's true.

Because everyone is unique, it's impossible to say exactly what your meditation will look like in precise terms. However, meditations generally fall into one of five categories—three of which are effective, two of which are not.

Please note that these examples are not either/or scenarios. You're probably going to experience all five of them during any one meditation. Also, the example that follows is not a real mantra, so don't try this at home.

When you sit down to meditate, your back is supported, your head is free, you check the time before you begin, and you do the math for your ending time—15 minutes for the mindfulness and meditation, then approximately 2 minutes of manifesting as you come out of your state of deep rest. Then, close your eyes and let that mantra come to you like a hot person in a bar.

EFFECTIVE MEDITATION EXPERIENCE #1:
THE THOUGHT TRAIN

You settle down for your meditation, taking a few seconds to simply chill with your eyes closed. Once you pick up your mantra and think it a few times, you then allow it to get fainter and finer like a whisper in the background of your mind, noticing how it may get longer or shorter, louder or softer, faster or slower, all on its own, after you've let it echo a few times. Eventually, it might separate from all meaning and simply become a sound. You start to think your mantra:

(Ziva.)[Yes, I am using the word *Ziva* as the prototype mantra in these examples.] (Ziva. Ziva. Ziiiva.) That's a weird word, Ziva. Weird. Word. Weird word. I wonder why *W* makes a "wuh" sound. *Wuh.* Hawaii. How do you pronounce Hawaii? "Hawai-*uh*"? Wait, no, I think it's actually "Hawai'i" with that glottal stop toward the end. Huh. Wuh. Woah, I wonder how much time has passed? Let me just check. Five minutes. Okay. That wasn't so bad. I bet I can do another five.

(Ziva. Ziva.) Diva. Ziva. Diva. Viva. Ziva diva viva. Ziva Las Vegas! That's not it, it's "Viva Las Vegas." Viva. (Ziva.) Huh. Oh, crap, I left money in my pants pocket. Do not forget that, money in my pants, money in my pants, money in my pants. Wait, how am I going to remember that? I know—that Ellen DeGeneres bit where she talks about "M in the P, M in the P, M in the P." Oh no, now I have to pee. Wait—Ellen is a meditator, isn't she? I wonder if I'm as good a meditator as she is. Um, am I judging my meditation against a celebrity? This doesn't feel very enlightened. That must've been five minutes. Let me just check. One minute. Well, okay, then. Back to the mantra.

Even if you're having thoughts and thoughts and thoughts and thoughts, provided that you sat down with the intention to meditate and let your mantra come to you like a faint, faint idea—and if you take the safety stop at the end—this is correct meditation. You are allowed to take mental field trips and go off on thought trains. You simply gently float back to that mantra when you realize you're off. ***Remember, thoughts are not the enemy of meditation; effort is. Thoughts are an indicator that stress is leaving the body.***

Also, keep in mind that anytime you're curious how much time has passed, you can simply open your eyes and check your watch or your clock or your phone (if it *has* to be your phone, make sure it's on airplane mode and that you've downloaded the app The Clocks; see page 131). If it's not your ending time (15 minutes for mindfulness and meditation, then an additional 2 for manifesting), just close your eyes and pick the mantra back up. Don't let your curiosity about the passage of time consume you. After a few days, you'll start to be amazed how accurate your internal clock is if you take the time to train it.

EFFECTIVE MEDITATION EXPERIENCE #2: THE PARTY

You sit down, your back is supported, your head is free, you check the time before you begin, you do the math, you close your eyes. You let the mantra come to you . . .

(Ziva. Ziva. Ziiiiivaaaa . . .) Oh, wow. You know what I need to get done this week? My taxes! Ugh, I do *not* want to wade through all my receipts. Although that will be a good way to do the homework from the book and tally up how much money stress is costing me. I need to make sure I get that on the schedule and—what was I doing again? Oh, right. Meditating. Excuse me, taxes, I need to go talk to my mantra . . . (Ziva . . . Ziva . . .) Should I get bangs? I really liked the bangs I saw on that woman at the store the other day. But would that style work with my face shape? I think it might, but am I ready for that much of a hair commitment? Wait—what was I supposed to be doing? Meditating! Excuse me, bangs, I need to go visit my mantra . . . (Ziva . . . Ziva . . .) I wonder what my dog is thinking about right now. Probably treats. Man, he loves treats. I wish I loved anything as much as my dog loves treats. If he had a mantra, I bet his mantra would be "Treats. Treats. Trrreats. Treats." That's not my mantra. What was my mantra? Oh, right. (Ziva.) Treats. (Ziva.) Treats. (Ziva . . .)

In this example, your mantra's gotten a little bit fainter and finer, but you have thoughts going on at the same time. You will find this happens much of the time. Here's how you want to handle thoughts and mantra happening simultaneously: Treat it like a party.

At this party, your mantra is the guest of honor and your thoughts are the guests. The invited guests are the thoughts you like having; the uninvited guests are the thoughts you don't like having. The invited guests are "I just got a raise at work," "I'm dating this amazing new person," "I think I'm the best meditator in the land," and so forth. The uninvited guests are "I don't know if I'm doing this right," "I don't like this mantra," "I feel like I'm wasting my time," "I have a thousand e-mails to answer," "I don't know how to make rent this month," and so on. These are your stupid, stressy, uninvited guests. *But here's the thing:* At this party, you're the host of the party, not the bouncer. I'll bet you're infinitely capable of going to a party and holding hands with your date—in this case, the guest of honor, the mantra—and having a conversation with plenty of other people at the same time.

Now, this party analogy is a good one. You're going to use it a lot. Some of the parties you're going to love—a collection of a few of your closest friends at an exquisite dinner party. Other meditations are going to be more like overcrowded frat parties with loud music, strobe lights, and a hundred drunk guys barfing on the lawn. Whatever kind of party your meditation ends up being, remember, you are the *host*, not the *bouncer*.

I want you to take this analogy pretty literally. Let's say you're at a party and you're talking to someone, and after a few moments you realize they're pretty annoying, with nothing interesting to say and some kickin' bad breath.

Rather than simply cutting them off and walking away rudely, you're going to let them finish their thought, then you will find a polite way to exit: "Oh, pardon me, I'm going to chat with an old friend," and then gracefully exit in that direction.

You turn and you go *toward* the positive, not *away* from the negative. The same thing is true in meditation. When you realize your thoughts have taken you off the mantra, turn your mind gently toward the mantra rather than steering your mind away from the thoughts.

EFFECTIVE MEDITATION EXPERIENCE #3: BLISS FIELD

The third thing that can happen during meditation is what I like to call the "bliss field." It looks a little something like this: You begin to meditate, pick up your mantra, and . . .

(Ziva. Ziva. Ziva. Ziva. Ziva. Ziva. . . . . .) (. . . . . .) (. . . . . .)
Woah! What just happened, I think I was supposed to be meditating. Okay, right. (Ziva. Ziva. Ziva. Ziva. Ziva. Ziva . . .)
(. . . . . .) (. . . . . .)

You have a momentary thought of, *Oh, wait, I'm off the mantra,* but the last thought you had was the mantra. There's this little space of time there that you can't really account for. Maybe you were drifting or maybe you were dozing or maybe it felt like sleeping. One minute felt like one hundred, or fifteen minutes felt like two. It's easy to confuse this with sleep. The thing is, it isn't sleep. This is the lazy man's meditation; you're actually falling into the bliss field—that fourth state of consciousness I've been telling you so much about.

Now, here's the trick about the bliss field: You're never going to know you're there *when* you're there. By definition, you've moved beyond the realm of thinking and into the realm of being, so you're never going to have a thought like, *Oh, yes, I'm currently in the bliss field and it's currently amazing.*

Normally, you know it right afterward when you're like, *Oh, wait, I think I was just doing it! I was just in the bliss field! Wait, now I want it back! Wait, Ziva, Ziva, Zivaaaaaaaaaaaa!* Then you start chasing the dragon a little bit, which is all normal in the first few days. What's going to get easier is just letting it come when it wants to and letting it last for as long as it needs to.

These first three examples are all perfectly splendid things to have happen during the meditation portion of the Z Technique, and you'll most likely experience all three during any given sitting.

Now let's move on to two things that commonly happen during meditation where you're going to want to course correct.

INEFFECTIVE MEDITATION EXPERIENCE #1: CONTEMPLATION

The fourth thing that can happen during meditation is contemplation. It looks a little something like this:

(Ziva. Ziva. Ziva. Ziva.) I wonder if I should go to the gym after work? Duh, yes, you should always go to the gym after work. You always feel better when you go. (Ziva. Ziva.) Oh, but I have a big work project due tomorrow. Oh, I should definitely finish that project. (Ziva.) But I really want to go to the gym, but I hate it when I'm there! Oh, if I go to the gym, I'm going to feel guilty about not doing this project. (Ziva. Ziva. Ziva.) Hang on, mantra. I need to figure this out. If I do this project, I'm going to feel guilty about not going to the gym. Argh! Should I finish my work or go to the gym? Work or work out? Work or work out? Oh, wait. I think I was supposed to be meditating. What was my mantra again? (Ziva.) I SAID TO WAIT A MINUTE, MANTRA! Work or work out? Work or work out?

In this example, you realize you're off the mantra, but you *choose* to stay off the mantra because you have to finish solving the great mystery of whether to work or work out. This is one of the few things we can do "wrong" in meditation. When you realize you're off the mantra and *choose* to stay off, this moves you from meditation into contemplation, and you have the other 23½ hours of your day to contemplate. You don't need to read this book in order to learn how to contemplate.

For these 15 minutes, twice a day, you're going to meditate, and all that means is that when you realize you're off the mantra, you easily, gently float back to it. Now, the trick about contemplation is that all these thoughts that are bubbling up are going to feel super relevant, super important, and super special; but 99.9 percent of the time, they're not. Most of the time, your brain is simply taking out the mental trash.

No need to have a journal next to you to write down every single thought that comes up. Just let it go and trust that amazing ideas are going to be flowing more freely in your waking state. Anything worth knowing will still be there for you after the meditation is over.

The only real difference between contemplation and the thought train is that in contemplation, you realize you're off the mantra and actively *choose* to remain off. In the thought train, once you realize you've wandered off the mantra, you simply allow yourself to drift back to it. It is 100 percent fine to have a thousand thoughts swirling around in your brain, but when your mantra starts tapping you on the shoulder, that means it's time to go back to the task at hand: namely, destressing. Do not ignore that or put it off.

INEFFECTIVE MEDITATION EXPERIENCE #2:
THE BASEBALL BAT

You settle down, close your eyes, pick up your mantra:

(Ziva . . . Ziva . . .) I wonder what my dog is thinking about right now. Probably treats. Man, he loves treats— NO! Shut up, brain! Not the treats again. ZIVA! ZIVA! ZIVA! I wish I loved anything as much as my dog loves— ZIVA! ZIIIIIVAAAAA!

The fifth thing that can happen during meditation is that we use the mantra like a baseball bat to whack the thoughts away. You start thinking, *Even though Emily said she's been meditating for more than eleven years and she's never had a thought-free meditation, I bet secretly she's over there swimming around in the bliss field the whole time, so anytime I have a thought, I'm just going to swat it away like I'm playing an intense game of Whac-A-Mole. I'm just going to be like,* mantra, mantra, mantra, mantra! *and knock out every single thought that comes near me.*

This experience stands in direct opposition to the concept of union attained by action hardly taken. Your mantra is not a baseball bat with which to beat back thoughts. Just as guests at a cocktail party would be (rightly) disturbed if you ran around bludgeoning them with a Louisville Slugger, you should treat both your mantra and your thoughts as guests. When you realize you've taken a mental field trip (which is allowed), gently float back to your mantra.

It's really tempting to use the baseball bat if you're in a noisy environment and you're judging those noises as bad or as a "distraction." It's understandable to want to use the mantra to bat away all the noise. Please don't do that. Just let the noise be part of the experience. Keep in mind that noise is no barrier to meditation. Anywhere you can think a thought, you can think the mantra. If you can think the mantra, you can meditate!

What you're going to find is that the less effort you use with the mantra, the more powerful it is. You're probably already noticing that if you start focusing or concentrating or furrowing your brow, you're going to start getting headaches right up in the prefrontal cortex, which is your brain training you more effectively than I ever could. But if you let the mantra be a whisper of an echo in the background of your mind, then it starts to act as an anchor and begins to de-excite the nervous system.

Basically, when you focus or concentrate on the mantra, your brain's going to punish you with headaches. If you use it like a feather, like a whisper of an echo to de-excite your nervous system, your brain is going to treat you with dopamine and serotonin. Isn't your brain so, so smart?

Here's the trick about the baseball bat. We usually use it when we are *trying* to get to the bliss field. The more you try to get there, the farther away you'll move from it. Know that accessing the bliss field is not the point or the goal. And it would be a terrible goal to have, because you would never know if you had accomplished it until you were already out of it again. The good news is that it doesn't matter how long you're in the bliss field because you're moving beyond the realm of thinking into the realm of being, which means you're moving beyond the realm of time. This is not the place to be competitive. You don't get any gold stars for staying in the bliss field for two extra minutes. That is not up to you. The bliss field is just one of the things that can happen during the cycle that is meditation. It is not the point, the goal, or the only time you are getting benefit. And paradoxically, the harder you try to access it, the further away you will get from it. So easy does it, friends. Give yourself permission to be sloppy, even lazy, with your practice. It will make you so much less lazy in the rest of your life.

» A Few Final Thoughts . . .

Just as you can't command your heart to stop beating or your mind to stop thinking, you can't will your brain into one type of sitting or another. Your body and mind will work together with your mantra to steer the unstressing process in whatever direction your body needs to go. The harder you try to control the experience, the less effective it's going to be; even if it runs counter to every high-achieving instinct you possess, the faster you accept that, the less "effort" you put into the actual act of meditating, the better it will be for you. Remember when we talked about surrender? This is where it becomes key: Your job is not to do anything at all, beyond keeping to the schedule of twice-a-day sittings within the framework I've laid out. Simply get your buns in the chair twice a day every day—and trust me, that is plenty challenging. Once you get to the chair, let the mantra take over. Trust that your body knows how to heal itself, and that you know how to give it the rest it needs. This is *nishkam karma yoga,* baby. Union attained by action *hardly* taken. This is your new program—twice a day every day.

The Z Technique Daily Program

1. Set your alarm to wake up 20 minutes earlier than usual.
2. Freshen up.
3. Hit the chair:
   - Back supported, head free.
   - Have a timepiece near you.
   - Don't worry if the room around you isn't silent.
   - Before you begin, know what time you want to come up and out. Do the math on your 15-minute end time.
   - **MINDFULNESS:** Start with 1 to 2 minutes of Come to Your Senses.
   - **MEDITATION:** Let the mantra come to you, gently. This is not a focusing tool, and thoughts are not the enemy—effortlessness is key. If the mantra doesn't bubble up on its own, pick it up as a faint idea. If it slips away, let it go. Other thoughts will come in. That is great. When you are curious how much time has passed, open your eyes and check your timepiece as often as you like. Don't set an alarm; start to train your internal clock. (If you like, you can set a backup alarm for 22 minutes as an extra precaution so you don't worry about sleeping through your whole day.)
   - **MANIFESTING:** In the 2-minute safety stop af-

ter you put down your mantra, take a moment of gratitude, then gently transition into visualizing a dream or goal as if it is happening right now. Give yourself the gift of feeling how you want to feel on the other side of the goal.

4. Enjoy the rest of your day at peak performance levels.

5. Rinse and repeat midafternoon/early evening. Until it becomes second nature, schedule your second meditation on your calendar as you would a call with your lawyer or a lunch date with your best friend.

6. Don't let perfect be the enemy of good. Don't let good be the enemy of done. Just get your buns to the chair twice a day and let the mantra do the rest.

HOMEWORK: Take out your phone or calendar and schedule your next twenty-one days of meditation. For real. It will only take you five minutes, but it will make or break your meditation career. If it isn't scheduled, it won't get done. Schedule your morning alarm for twenty minutes earlier than you usually wake up so you have time to do your morning practice before breakfast. Then look at each day and decide where on your oh-so-full calendar you will prioritize yourself, your brain, and your performance.

You can't pour from an empty cup, so get in the habit of making yourself a priority. Trust me, everyone else will thank you.

BETTER PARKING KARMA

CONGRATULATIONS! YOU'VE DONE YOUR RESEARCH, YOU'RE committed to this journey, and you're ready to see your performance improve in every area of your life. Here's where things start to get especially interesting: After a few weeks of twice-a-day sittings and once you've moved through the initial phases of mental and physical detox, you will probably notice the effects of your Z Technique beginning to extend beyond the workplace and spill over into your everyday life. This is a phenomenon I have affectionately dubbed "better parking karma," and it's real. Don't be freaked out by the sudden uptick in "coincidences" in your life—it simply means the effects of your daily discipline and action of getting into the chair are beginning to permeate your body, mind, and performance.

» Rumble Strips on the Road of Life

I want to clarify what I mean by *karma*. In the West, the concept has generally been used to reference a kind of cosmic bank account, where the good you do to or for others is eventually paid back to you, and any bad you experience is the result of negative actions from your past that have to be burned off to reset the balance. This is a misconception, however; a literal translation of the Sanskrit word *karma* is "action." When I talk about improving your parking karma, I'm not referring to the payback of good deeds on your soul or what the universe owes you or any kind of punishment for something done in the past. Karma is simply the actions you take and the ripple effect of those actions in your life.

KARMA: Literally translated, *karma* simply means "action."

DHARMA: Your life's path or journey.

(It should be noted that these terms link back to the ancient wisdom contained in the Vedas. The Vedas are a human interpretation of the laws of Nature and are not a religious dogma or doctrine.)

Dharma, on the other hand, is the Sanskrit word used to describe your life's path or greater purpose. The way karma and dharma work together can be illustrated by thinking about driving down a nicely paved six-lane highway. Dharma is the actual trajectory of your trip, while karma is either the smooth flow of traffic that allows you to arrive at your destination with ease and elegance, or the rumble strips on the shoulder, there to wake you up and get you back in your lane if you start to swerve off your path.

If we look at karma in this way—as gentle bumps to let us know when we are off course, or serendipity to affirm we are on our path—we can better understand how the effects of adding mindfulness, meditation, and manifesting into your day can spread far beyond the boundaries of your professional or personal life. As your consciousness expands, you'll likely begin to notice more and more happy "coincidences" in your life, whether it's finding parking at exactly the right time, or making connections with people who perfectly match desires you (or they) have been wanting to fulfill. This beautiful symphony of serendipity and synchronicity is a blending of your deepening intuition combined with the fog of neediness being wiped from the lens of your understanding. As your confidence in trusting your own instincts and inner voice grows, you'll begin to find that your actions become more decisive and meaningful, even if you aren't always initially sure of the reasoning behind them. I call this strengthening of your intuition, or Nature's GPS.

Let's revisit the concept of simultaneity of consciousness. As you continue to commit to your twice-a-day sittings, your increased ability to hold multiple things in one awareness will allow you to pick up on subtle, almost imperceptible clues, which, in turn, will allow you to read situations faster and with more accuracy. You may subconsciously begin recognizing and internalizing patterns for when your favorite businesses are less busy, meaning better parking and shorter lines. Your mental directory of facts about people's lives may start improving, so you're suddenly finding that seemingly unrelated acquaintances actually have resources and goals that align, thus enabling each to accomplish more. In other words, the life you up-level may not only be your own.

» Follow Charm

The best advice I can give to people who find themselves noticing an uptick in serendipity is simply to "follow charm"; in other words, *go with your gut*. That is the beauty of honing your intuition: You will grow increasingly confident in trusting where it leads you. This kind of intuition allows you to read situations as they are and act accordingly, rather than trying to force one course of events or another. When we detach ourselves from the outcome, we allow things to be as they are rather than as we force them to be. By no means am I advocating that you merely become a passive observer of life; rather, I want you to give yourself permission to encounter the world authentically and deliver your fulfillment to the real needs you are uniquely positioned to meet. When things feel serendipitous, that is karma indicating that you're delivering your fulfillment exactly where you're meant to. And because of your ever-expanding ability to recognize subtlety, you'll also have an ever-expanding ability to provide solutions and connections.

Let me share a personal example. One sunny day a few years ago, I was walking to work at Ziva in New York City when I suddenly found myself having a serious "download" for chocolate. I am all too familiar with what a chocolate addiction looks like. This was different; it was Nature downloading a desire. I paused for just a moment to marvel at what a weird sensation it was to come on so suddenly and be so strong—I wasn't pregnant, and I don't have much of a sweet tooth anymore, but I could not shake the feeling that I absolutely had to have chocolate ASAP. I doubled back to step into the bakery I had just passed, thinking maybe something in there would take care of the craving, and found myself face-to-face with an old friend of mine named Pam. I was thrilled to see her, as we had fallen out of touch over the past few years, and we ended up spending some time catching up. Pam and I had done a national tour of *The Producers* together, and she was now a licensed massage therapist, but she shared that she had recently done a yoga teacher training and was feeling a desire to combine her massage and yoga in some way. She was struggling with finding a direction that felt right, and I suggested that she look into Ayurveda, as there are branches of it that incorporate elements of both touch and yoga. She lit up at the suggestion and said that was exactly the sort of direction she had wanted to go, but hadn't been sure of the right path. I immediately put her in touch with my Ayurvedic doctor, and she is now training to be a practitioner.

After we hugged good-bye and went our separate ways, I realized that my chocolate craving had gone away, and I hadn't even had so much as a bite of a brownie. That's when I realized that the craving had never been about me getting chocolate at all; it had simply been my brain's way of getting my attention, or Nature's way of cuing me as to where it wanted to use me to share a gift. Perhaps I saw Pam through the window as I passed, but since it had been such a long time since we had seen each other, I didn't consciously register that I knew her. Perhaps there was something bigger at play. In order to trigger my body to turn around, my mind cued an overwhelming craving to get me inside that bakery so I would recognize and re-connect with an old friend. And as a result of that "chance" meeting, I was able to offer my knowledge of Ayurvedic medicine and help Pam get on the smoothly paved road of her dharma. What seemed like nothing more than a chocolate craving was really my intuition steering me to an opportunity to deliver my fulfillment to a friend so that she could find her own fulfillment in turn. The key here is a shift in perception.

The habitual reaction, when faced with hard times, is "Why is this happening **to** *me?" What I would encourage you to think instead is, "Why is this happening* **for** *me?"* Going back to the image of the rumble strips on the side of the highway, what is the better reaction: to bemoan the fact that you're driving over the loud, bumpy things, or to recognize the warning they are issuing you and course correct? The same principle is at work here. When you shift your focus from things happening *to* you (making you a victim) to recognizing that they are happening *for* you (for your growth, development, and ultimate strengthening), you not only take back your power in life but also come to recognize the much bigger implications and echoes of your actions. There is both a cause for the event you're experiencing right now and a lesson to be learned from it—past, present, and future all coming together to help you evaluate your current reality. (Thank goodness your right brain is getting strong enough to hold its own alongside leftie, huh?) As you continue to let the belief that things are happening *for* you—that God, Nature, the universe, or whatever higher power you believe in is on your side and using karma as a way to guide you toward your higher purpose—you'll find it gets easier to discover the lesson and direction in every circumstance. When we see the rough patches in life as guidance rather than punishment, we start to ask better questions. And as you follow charm (that is, listen to your gut) as it leads you toward the beautiful surprises life has in store for you, whether it's something as seemingly insignificant as an open table at a popular restaurant or as major as a chance encounter with the executive you've been trying to get a meeting with for six months, you'll find that *you are an influencer in the world, and the world you influence is so much bigger than you realize*.

» Flow State

A concept that has been gaining a lot of traction in recent years is what is commonly known as "flow state." The term was coined by psychologist Mihály Csíkszentmihályi to describe the mental state in which a person has seemingly supernatural intuition, sometimes to the point of losing a sense of time, that results in tremendous accomplishment at a very high level. Athletes call it "being in the zone." You've probably experienced it yourself—you started working on a project, performance, or physical feat, and time seemed to stand still or slow down and your instincts became finely tuned. You may have even felt like you were outside yourself as you managed to succeed again and again, topping your previous performance each time. Flow state usually only lasts a few minutes, a few hours, tops, but what you can accomplish within that short span of time tends to dwarf your accomplishments when you're outside of flow state.

The idea is nothing new; it has been a recognized part of Eastern thinking for thousands of years—the human brain can generate tremendous results when it's able to access higher states of consciousness beyond the basic waking state. When a person's brain kicks into that higher mode of operation, it's firing rapidly, churning out ideas and executing movements, but without the hindrance of self-consciousness or doubt. Remember back in chapter 4 when we discussed the alpha and theta waves that help the brain transition from waking to sleeping? Studies have found that alpha and theta waves take over when a person enters flow state as well. Have you ever marveled at the creativity of your dreams, or woken up thinking, *That would make such a good movie/novel/product/idea?* When you're in that in-between state, not quite dreaming, you don't have that left-brain, critical voice of inhibition to make you second-guess yourself or to tell you that whatever you're dreaming can't be done.

But how do we tap into flow state? There are two ways. The first is simply to start working on something, cross your fingers, and hope really hard that flow state comes. But as my brilliant husband often reminds me, hope is not a strategy. If hoping for flow state was all it took to bring it on, we would all be slipping into it every time we stepped onstage, sat down to work, went for a jog, or attempted anything at all. For most of us, our brains are not trained to dip into this in-between state without either jerking back into full, waking consciousness or else drifting straight into sleep.

The second way to access flow state is to train your body and mind to easily enter into and then substantiate that state of consciousness into your waking state. And the way to do that is—wait for it—a regular meditation practice. (Oh, come on. You had to know that was coming.)

Meditation produces the same alpha and theta waves in the brain that almost-sleep and flow state produce. The longer you cultivate a daily practice, the more innocently you'll start to access that place of extraordinary creativity, innovation, and execution. The more comfortable you get with allowing your brain to explore that space, the more seamless and natural it will be to tap into it even when you're not in a meditation session. And if you choose to pursue even deeper forms of meditation as part of your personal journey, you'll likely find that flow state becomes your new norm.

One of the ways you can deepen your practice, if that feels charming, is to dive into our fifteen-day online training, zivaONLINE, at www.zivameditation.com/online. One of the graduates of the online training shared with me that her body feels like a new Google self-driving car and she doesn't have to drive anymore. Talk about mastering flow!

This is what another zivaONLINE student, Larry Sark, shared about his experience with flow, offering some powerful words of encouragement for you as you start your journey:

As a recovering perfectionist and workaholic, zivaONLINE has changed my life. I started a few months ago and made the twice-daily practice of the 3 M's a nonnegotiable part of my life. I have been through emotionally challenging times since then. However, I am much more in flow, patient, and flexible in life. I am more focused and productive at work. I get more done in less time, which means work doesn't occupy my entire *life anymore. I am now able to enjoy life even more. If you are just starting, this is a game changer. Please give yourself the time you need to get used to it and make meditation a part of your daily routine. The people around you will thank you.*

But how does your ability to more easily tap into flow state affect the world around you? When you're tapped into something bigger than yourself, not only does it allow you to perform at a higher level, but you also free up more of your time and energy to help other people and inspire them to up-level their own performance. What most of us truly desire is the experience we think we will have once we achieve our goals: freedom, fulfillment, comfort. You need to ask yourself whether it's more satisfying to chase those feelings by pursuing empty stuff or to earn them through your performance in your job and in life, and how you can in turn convert that success into better decisions that will impact your family, your company, your community, and even the planet at large.

» Change the World, 15 Minutes at a Time

I know you may be a whopping two days into your meditation career right now, so healing the world may feel like it's a few steps away, but I want to give you a preview of coming attractions. How can sitting quietly in a chair twice a day impact the world? On a small scale, I can say with confidence that when you start meditating, you become much more intuitive about what your body is actually asking for to perform at peak efficiency. Something as simple as getting more in tune with your body's demands can change the way you eat, shop, move, think, and connect with other people. On a bigger scale, it's worth noting that the same connection that makes you more empathetic also makes you more generous. When you meditate, you light up something called the dorsomedial prefrontal cortex, which is the part of your brain that processes information about people we perceive as different. You also strengthen the connection between the dorsomedial prefrontal cortex and the insula, which is the empathy center of the brain. The result is that you become more empathetic toward people you perceive as different.

This can also have the effect of making you more generous. When the neurotransmitters that help these parts of the brain communicate are strengthened, people become better able to feel and to give. If you move out of the "I'll be happy when . . ." syndrome and allow meditation to remind you that your happiness can never be found externally, then your relationship with your desires changes. You may still want to make a lot of money, but you'll no longer be under the illusion that piles of money are going to make you happy. You will instead allow your desires to be indicators of where Nature is using you to deliver your fulfillment along the way to your desires. This helps you transition from old feelings of greed and lack to ones of abundance and generosity.

In fact, in a scientific study,[1] meditators were proven to act with more generosity than nonmeditators. When we shift our primary focus from acquiring gobs of money to delivering fulfillment, we help nudge the needle of our cultural thinking little by little away from scarcity thinking, which is what fuels greed, into a mind-set of abundance, which fuels generosity.

Most of us are familiar with the old adage from Gandhi, "Be the change you wish to see in the world." But this lesser-known Gandhi quote perfectly sums up the point I want to make: "As human beings, our greatness lies not so much in being able to remake the world . . . but in being able to remake ourselves." When we personally grow our empathy, we grow our capacity for love and shrink our capacity for anything that opposes that empathy.

The Dalai Lama said, "If we were to teach every eight-year-old to meditate, we would end war within a generation." Does your decision to begin a meditation practice somehow mean that someone seven thousand miles away will suddenly be inspired to begin one, too? No. But your decision is increasing the world's capacity for empathy, even if just by one person. And that is significant. As you heal yourself, you help to heal the collective.

The reasons you choose to begin your meditation journey are your own, and the results that come of it are going to impact your own life most of all. But what you choose to do with those results—the decrease in your stress, the increase in your health and creative energy, your expanded consciousness and increasing empathy, your developing intuition and sense of fulfillment—has the potential to create a legacy of impact that will resonate far beyond your own life and potentially even your own lifetime.

Eyes-Closed Exercise

Superpower Pose

While writing this book I often imagine stress as the villain, you as the hero, and these powerful mental techniques as your new superpower. In this exercise we're going to activate the brain, the breath, and the body to get into the mind space of success right off the bat. Our body language is affected by our mental state, and conversely, our mental state is affected by our body language, so let's create the physical posture of victory so we can get into that mental state. Start by bringing your arms over your head to make a giant V shape or what referees do to signal a touchdown. Make sure your palms are open and facing each other.

Holding this pose, we are going to start something called "breath of fire," a fast in/out through the nostrils. Begin by softening your jaw; let your lips part. Soften your brow and begin to quickly inhale and exhale through both nostrils at the same time. You can start slow, but eventually you want to build up to a quick pace as if you are an excited, panting puppy. (But pant through your nostrils, not your mouth.)

Breathe quickly for 30 seconds, softening the face and letting the impulse for the breath start with the belly. If you take a peek at your belly, you should see it quickly rising and falling. Your arms may start to ache a little, and that's okay. If you're standing and start to feel light-headed, you may want to sit down. (This will all get easier the more you practice.)

Now lower your arms, close your eyes, and take a moment to check in. What is the most prevalent body sensation happening right now? How do you feel now compared with how you felt before you started? Can you feel the blood flowing back into your arms? Take a moment to assimilate that feeling of joy and victory into every cell of your body.

Begin again. Bring your arms over your head into the V shape, palms open and facing each other. Now begin the breath of fire again, this time for 45 seconds.

Allow yourself to be a vessel for Nature to work through you. Imagine yourself as a channel for energy, ideas, and intuition to flow through. Get your ego, your doubts, and your attachment to outcome out of the way. You are simply the conductor. Picture yourself as a giant antenna with energy entering your body through your arms and the top of your head, traveling down your body, and grounding through your feet. Enjoy the simultaneity of lightness and groundedness happening in your body right now, then finish the breath of fire and drop your arms.

Take another moment to substantiate that sensation and see how you feel different from when you started. Do this exercise as needed when you desire a confidence boost or ahead of a big event.

For a demonstration and guidance on this, visit www .zivameditation.com/bookbonus.

THE MOST AMAZING VERSION OF YOU

I'M GOING TO ASK YOU SOMETHING RATHER BLUNT: WHAT matters most in terms of your work performance? Are you evaluated and potentially promoted based on how you *feel about* your job or how you actually *perform* your job? This, I believe, is one of the most important questions to consider as you decide if it is worth it for you to commit to doing your daily Z Technique or not.

I hear from countless potential students that they are curious but ultimately reluctant to try because they are "too busy" or simply don't like the idea of becoming "one of those meditation types." That's good, because at Ziva we aren't really into that, either. In fact, most of our students come to us looking for a tool to improve their performance rather than a way to become a "meditation type." It really doesn't matter how you feel about meditation itself. I'd encourage you to consider this: Does anyone care how they feel during the forty-eighth minute on the Stairmaster? Does anyone really give a second thought to whether or not they're really enjoying the eight glasses of water they drink a day? Of course not. But what people *do* care about is whether their blood pressure is down and they have more energy. What you probably care about is whether your clothes fit you better, if your skin is more radiant, and if your mind is sharper. In other words, how you *feel* about the process of pursuing physical health doesn't matter; all that ultimately matters are the real results that come from those lifestyle changes.

The same is true of meditation. If you decide that all you really need to improve your life is a different workout routine or a public speaking course or a cleaner diet, or even if you decide that all this talk about less stress and better performance is hooey, I'm not going to know the difference.

But you will.

You are the person who has to live with the decisions you make each day. Maybe those other changes really will do the trick for you, and if that's the case, I wish you all the happiness in the world—truly. But if you've tried the same old changes before without lasting success, maybe it's time to try something else.

If your professional life is stagnant or your home life feels stuck in a rut, or if you feel a mental block that ingenuity simply cannot permeate, you can wait . . . but for what?

Maybe new opportunities will land in your lap. Maybe that brilliant idea will suddenly come to you in a flash of genius. Maybe your health will magically improve. Maybe your muscle tone will increase and your cholesterol count will decrease and you'll instantly become a paragon of physical fitness. Maybe your years of accumulated stress will all magically dissolve one day. Maybe things will get better by waiting. Maybe . . . but probably not.

You can wish for a new and improved version of you to live a new and improved version of your life, or you can do something new. As the saying goes, "The definition of insanity is doing the same thing over and over again, but expecting different results." You are not insane—you're amazing. You just have to be willing to trust yourself to cultivate that amazingness. One of my other favorite quotes is from Albert Einstein, who reportedly said, "No problem can be solved at the same state of consciousness with which it was created."

If you're having some lingering problems you haven't been able to solve for a while, maybe now is the time to try a practice that has been scientifically proven to increase your cognitive performance and up-level your state of consciousness. Now is the time to decide and commit. Make a promise to yourself and keep it. Every time you do, you build personal integrity.

» The Lowdown on Up-Leveling

In the realm of video games, "leveling up" means that a character has somehow won, achieved, or otherwise gained a higher level of success within the electronic world, which results in gaining new skills, new tools, or entry to other areas of the game. In other words, the character becomes a more advanced version of themselves.

In the real world, this same process has recently come to be known as "up-leveling." An "up-leveler" (as we say at Ziva) is simply someone who wants to be better every day—someone who is committed to learning, growth, and cultivating their skill set or competencies to the point that they are able to access higher echelons of performance, contribution, and accomplishment.

I can see you rolling your eyes. *Come on, Emily. Isn't that just a fancy new term for* self-help? Nope. Up-leveling is not just about improving self, it's about getting better at *life*—and not just your own life but the lives of people around you. Like the old expression goes, "A rising tide lifts all boats." When you begin to up-level your life, the people around you can't help but benefit from your increased productivity, insight, wisdom, confidence, and empathy. They, in turn, become inspired and empowered to up-level their own lives.

I mean, who wouldn't want to enjoy the benefits of being an

up-leveler? Getting better at literally everything while also becoming a better person? *Um, yes, please. I'll take two.* But up-leveling isn't an accident; you have to be willing to lay the foundation that makes it possible. And it doesn't just *happen;* you have to invest yourself in the process in order to yield the benefits. ***Up-leveling is not a stroke of luck; it's a choice.*** When I use the term *up-levelers,* I'm referring not to people who stumbled into success (we all know at least one of those). I'm talking about people who actively and deliberately made the choice to raise their performance in life from one level to a higher one. Up-levelers are dedicated not just to pursuing short-term goals but to raising the quality of every aspect of their mind, body, relationships, and interactions with the world.

That is why I beat the drum of Mindfulness, Meditation, and Manifesting so steadily. These mental techniques offer the highest yield with the least amount of effort of any behavioral practice I know. If you want to up-level your life and enjoy all the benefits doing so brings to you and those around you, you have to be willing to do the work to break yourself out of some old patterns. All our habits bear reexamining periodically to make sure they are still consistent with our current beliefs, priorities, and goals. That is one of the hallmarks of a successful individual in any field: a willingness to adapt habits in a continual effort to improve. You can stay where you are, as you are, altering nothing about yourself but hoping that things will somehow change for you. Or you can make small but purposeful adaptations—just a few adjustments or tweaks to your daily schedule—and begin to see deep, fundamental changes and improvements in how you think, how you perceive the world, and who you are as a human being.

The choice is ultimately up to you, but as the saying goes, a year from now, you'll wish you'd begun today.

» The Genius in Your Genes

Speaking of Einstein, he was just one of an impressive list of geniuses who seemed to grasp the significance of short, scheduled periods of rest during the day. Leonardo da Vinci famously followed a rather strange sleep pattern: Instead of going to bed at night, as is the current cultural norm, he instead opted to nap for fifteen or twenty minutes every four hours, around the clock. Sometimes he would sneak in slightly longer rests, but never more than two hours.

This practice, known as polyphasic sleeping, is a pretty extreme— almost manic—approach to slumber. But Aristotle, Albert Einstein, Thomas Edison, Nikola Tesla, and Salvador Dalí also engaged in brief, scheduled periods of repose during the day as a means of rejuvenating their minds and unblocking their ingenuity. Einstein was rumored to take twenty-minute "naps" when he couldn't solve a problem, then come back to look at it from a fresh angle. This suggests to me that although he may not have had access to these particular techniques borne out of ancient India, he was cognizing his own way to access *turiya,* or that fourth state of consciousness. In fact, the writings of visionary inventor Tesla demonstrate that he was very familiar with the Vedas and the wisdom contained inside.[1]

No, I am not claiming that all of these visionaries were practiced meditators (that we know of, anyway), nor am I implying that you, too, will be able to peek behind the curtain of space and time if you just follow the Z Technique. (Though if you do, it would be awesome if you could give us a shout-out in your Nobel Prize acceptance speech!) But I *am* saying that the annals of history are full of extraordinary men and women who understood the importance of short periods of rejuvenating rest during the day as part of the creative process. Modes of thinking that are out of the ordinary require preparation that is out of the ordinary. More recently, Harvard Medical School psychiatry professor Srini Pillay suggested that we need to schedule time for our brains to *un*focus every day so that we can better focus when needed.[2] His research indicates that the brain experiences focus fatigue with our modern schedules. While Pillay suggests taking a nap, I would offer that the Z Technique is exactly the sort of restful activity that has no agenda to focus on and will provide a welcome respite from focus fatigue without giving you the sleep hangover that naps are famous for.

Between one and ten minutes after you lie down to rest, the brain begins to send out sleep spindles, which are bursts of brain activity as the mind begins to power down. At roughly the twenty-minute mark, the brain begins to produce theta waves, which indicate that it's fully engaged in dreaming. Meditation, though different from napping, works with this same pattern of brain activity, allowing your body to get deep rest while the mind dips into this place that is beyond full waking consciousness but not yet in sleep.

If the idea of polyphasic sleep sounds as wildly inconvenient to you as it does to me, perhaps it's worth exploring alternatives that operate under comparable, but far less extreme, principles. That, I believe, is the beauty of this practice: It is a productivity and creativity tool that allows you to unlock higher levels of functioning without disrupting your entire way of being, along with those of your family, neighbors, coworkers, and clients. *Meditation allows you to up-level your life without up*ending *it.*

The list of geniuses I named above all recognized the value of cultivating short, practiced periods of repose. Of course, it's impossible to prove their rest patterns directly contributed to their brilliant insight and output, but it certainly seems more than coincidental that some of the most extraordinary thinkers in history all followed variations on this pattern of behavior.

When we look at that impressive list of names, it's easy to think, *Yeah, but they're geniuses. I mean, I may be smarter than the average bear or my idiot brother-in-law, but there is no way I'm like those guys.* The good news is, it doesn't matter if you're the next da Vinci or Tesla; you're uniquely positioned to impact the world with your own set of competencies, experiences, instincts, and ideas. Chances are, you're pretty exceptional at something. And if you want to develop your own genius and drive your personal success, what better way than to study the habits of great geniuses of the past to see if there is something there worth imitating?

In 2016, *Biological Psychiatry Journal* published a study conducted by a team led by J. David Creswell, assistant professor in the Department of Psychology and the Center for the Neural Basis of Cognition at Carnegie Mellon University.[3] What they found was that meditation decreased systemic inflammation in highly stressed job-seekers while increasing attention spans and improving the mental factors that control how a person behaves while trying to achieve a goal. In other words, meditation actually changed the way people thought about and dedicated themselves to achieving success, while also improving their physical health.

For those high achievers already in positions of authority and influence, the benefits of meditation are notable as well. After a fifteen-minute meditation, people made more confident and sound business decisions, according to a series of experiments conducted by an international team of researchers, which included a professor from the Wharton School of Business.[4]

Both our anecdotal evidence at Ziva and scientific evidence point to the fact that meditative rest seems to have a direct correlation to an improvement in our mental capacities and competencies, as well as a broadening effect on our ingenuity and creative problem-solving abilities. But *why?*

» Insight and Intuition

One of the biggest benefits of meditation is something we don't talk about much because of how profoundly hippie-dippie it sounds: the expansion of consciousness.

Before you toss this book aside, thinking, *I was with you up to this point, but now we're just getting into ridiculousness*, I'd like to take a moment to talk about what consciousness is in terms that don't sound like I moonlight selling patchouli from the back of a VW bus.

CONSCIOUSNESS: The animating force inside all of us; the quality or state of being aware, especially of something within oneself.

Every living thing is expressing consciousness, but to varying degrees. For my dog, expanded consciousness might look like a realization that while there is one person offering a snack, there is a second one offering a belly rub—and then having to decide which person to go to. No great moral implications there. But for humans, when I talk about expanding consciousness, what I mean is our awareness of how we connect with the world and our place in it. The more consciousness a person has, the more joy, peace, equanimity, and connectedness that person will enjoy. Less consciousness can create more suffering and more feelings of isolation.

There are three telltale signs of how much consciousness you have:

1. The ability to hold many things in one awareness—that is, to be mentally engaged on multiple levels effortlessly

2. The ability to detect subtleties
3. The ability to detect themes

How you perform in each of these matters has a direct impact on your personal and professional achievements. Consider, for example, your ability to hold many things in one awareness, or pull the lens back. Are you able to manage one project while pursuing leads and pitching ideas for the next one? Are you able to run a board meeting and be acutely aware of the hard facts of the negotiations while simultaneously noticing the emotional dynamics at play in the room? If you say yes, chances are that you're headed for the corner office more quickly than the person who melts down when pulled off task by a simple question. Are you able to operate your car, drink your coffee, put the address of the soccer fields into your GPS, and keep your kids and the carpoolers in your back seat under some semblance of order while you mentally reflect on your tasks for this week? If so, you're the superparent that all the other moms and dads marvel at.

Now think back to one of those days when you could barely manage one or two of those tasks at a time without freaking out, spilling your coffee, or forgetting something important you were supposed to be doing. Of course we're all going to have bad days when nothing seems to go our way, but when your default setting is effortlessly holding many things in one awareness because you have the mental space from eradicating useless stress, you're destined for a different kind of success.

And how does meditation accomplish this? When the right and left hemispheres of the brain are communicating with each other easily and effectively, your ability to work in the present while also dealing with whatever from the past or future is also knocking at your door will naturally improve. No matter what your job is, this ability to effectively pull the lens back on your scope of awareness is a highly beneficial skill.

What about the ability to detect subtleties? Why does it matter? In more common phrasing, this is a factor in your intuition. Those gut reactions and automatic judgment calls that inexplicably but undeniably tell you which way you ought to go don't come out of nowhere—they are the result of your mind detecting and registering sometimes extremely subtle pieces of information that act like clues pointing you in the right direction.

No two things are the same. No two potential relationships, no two job applicants, no two ideas, no two proposals for a client, not even two grapefruits at the grocery store. Life is giving us a constant stream of decisions to make. As we discussed in chapter 7, the more we meditate, the less likely we are to make a mistake. Remember, a mistake is a "miss-take"—we took something to be one thing when in actuality, it was something else. Mistakes happen when we overlook something or make a judgment call that is clouded by longing.

In a professional setting, finely honed intuition can be the key to success. Truly great leaders often seem to have a knack for when to take a gamble and when to play it safe; when to take someone at their word and when to call a bluff; when to trust someone and when to cut ties. For some people, intuition is a gift; for others, it's a skill they must actively cultivate. Either way, the ability to detect subtle differences in a more precise and accurate way is always an essential element in up-leveling your performance. When you use meditation to access your fulfillment internally, you erase that fog of longing; you clear the way for your perception to become keener and more consistently accurate.

Finally, let's consider the ability to detect themes. How conscious are we of the themes at work around us every day? A theme is simply a pattern, and people, families, organizations, Nature—they are working in patterns all the time. Now, it's pretty easy to detect other people's patterns. We are all experts when it comes to our roommate or our best friend's love life. We all have friends who call us at eleven P.M. for the fourth time that year, crying because they've been through yet another breakup or they've made yet another terrible life choice, and from where you sit, you can see plain as day the series of actions and decisions that they have engaged in that has put them in this same place yet again (or even deeper in the same hole).

But what about the ability to detect our *own* themes? How good are we, without the aid of a lot of counseling and a couple of major breakthroughs, at picking up on the patterns—in the choices we make, the actions we take, the relationships we develop or discard—in our own lives? Perhaps more than either of the other two attributes of higher states of consciousness, this is the one that has the greatest ramifications on both our professional and personal success.

As you continue to meditate, destress your nervous system, strengthen your right-and-left-brain balance, and sharpen your intuition, you will begin to feel your mental lens pull back to give you a wider scope of all the subtle details clamoring for your attention at once. In other words, you begin to see the forest rather than the trees. As your consciousness expands, you will be better able to recognize, identify, and name the patterns that have helped to craft the life you have right now. This understanding will allow you to put your time and attention on the themes that are constructive and take away your energy and resources from the themes that are destructive.

Expanded consciousness, you see, is not about mind trips with cosmic visions or dancing naked in the woods to become one with Nature—at least, not the way we're exploring it in this book. (And if that's your thing, you do you.) What the Z Technique will help you achieve is an awareness and elegance as you navigate the unending demands of your work life, home life, social life, and love life. You will find yourself handling your multitude of responsibilities with more grace and greater effectiveness. You will be more keenly attuned to the little clues that point you toward the best decisions, and you'll be more able to spot and eliminate damaging patterns while fostering positive ones. This ability to view the world through both ends of the telescope—the big-picture patterns and the microscopic details—is the ultimate key to becoming the most amazing version of you.

» Stop the Apology Addiction

Before we close this chapter, I'd like to look at how the expansion of consciousness you are now developing can help you move from downplaying your own abilities to celebrating your best self with no sense of guilt, apology, or backpedaling. As you start meditating, your "deserving power" increases. Deserving power is what you secretly believe you deserve. As you know, we don't get what we want in life—we get what we believe we deserve. Over time, this increase in deserving power will help you break the apology addiction.

DESERVING POWER: What you believe you deserve.

Not long ago, a friend invited me over for dinner. She asked me to bring my favorite bottle of wine to pair with a special meal she was preparing. She'd been hungry to test out a new recipe and thought I would be the perfect guinea pig.

I arrived promptly at seven P.M., excited to try some delicious new cuisine that my friend had prepared with *so* much love. She invited me in and opened the entirely-too-expensive-for-a-screwtop wine I had brought. The timer went off, and when she presented her stunningly crafted meal, she placed it down on the table and immediately said, "I'm so sorry. This just didn't turn out how I wanted it to. It's probably terrible. It's okay—you can tell me if it's terrible. I won't be offended. I'm not really much of a chef anyway."

I hadn't even had a chance to try the dish she had worked so hard to prepare, and already she felt as if she needed to ask forgiveness for the possibility that it might be less than perfect.

I used to do this all the time. I spent most of my teens and twenties apologizing constantly for things that were not my fault or even preemptively apologizing for something I'd created for someone else. This is a common trait in children of alcoholics. I don't like to stereotype by gender, but I know from personal experience and from watching thousands of students that this tends to be something women struggle with more than men. Thankfully, as I began to grow in my practice, I was able to curb this behavior, but I know it's still a rampant problem for many of us.

When we create something—whether it's dinner for a friend, a presentation at work, a self-published memoir, or a new company—we are, by definition, bringing something from the un-manifest into the manifest. We're stepping into the unknown and making ourselves vulnerable by putting into concrete terms something we had nurtured in our mind, which leaves our ideas and ourselves subject to other people's judgment. That can be incredibly scary and lead to a less-than-elegant plague of self-consciousness and doubt. We often end up apologizing for our work, our choices, and even our very existence when someone bumps into us in the grocery store.

Here's the reality: When faced with a deadline, important project, or creative challenge, none of us feel as if we have enough time or enough resources. I don't know one creative person who has birthed something and then dropped the internal mic without a second thought. Most of us are constantly trying to figure out how we are lacking and how we can improve next time. That can make you feel really vulnerable, but it doesn't give you permission to apologize for your work. So here is your challenge, if you choose to accept it: Don't preface your future unveilings (of any kind) by pointing out and obsessing over every tiny flaw. You may judge something as imperfect, but others might not view it that way at all. When you apologize preemptively, you're giving them permission to lead with disapproval.

And my friend's dish, by the way, ended up being utterly delectable. Her worry and stress were for nothing; the whole meal tasted divine. But even if it hadn't been great, we still enjoyed a wonderful evening of friendship and laughs together. That experience by itself would have made up for any failings in the food. And my hypothesis is that if she hadn't preemptively apologized for something that did not need forgiveness, it may have tasted even sweeter. When we criticize our creations while presenting them, we are actually insulting the recipient if they enjoy it. Rude.

We all know that one of the most important elements of success is confidence—whether real or projected. No one wants to follow a shaky leader who second-guesses their own decisions and abilities. When I learned to meditate, I found a new and very different sense of confidence and trust in myself. This allowed me to snuff out my apology addiction pretty quickly. As I learned to hold multiple things in one awareness, I became much better at meeting all my obligations with a higher degree of proficiency; this gave me a stronger sense of my own capabilities. As I learned to trust my intuition, I found the confidence in my choices growing daily. And as I became more adept at detecting patterns in both myself and others, I felt my insight and creativity grow as I found new solutions and new ideas that took my life and my career in a direction I knew was going to have a powerful impact.

There is a second aspect to this, however, and that is to break the addiction to *trying*. In the famous words of Yoda, "Do or do not. There is no try."

Trying is an attempt to achieve something. Are you *trying* to be successful? *Trying* to get in shape? *Trying* to save money? *Trying* to meditate? If the answer is yes, congratulations! You've made it. It's happening now. You are currently succeeding *at trying*.

The thing is, though, trying isn't enough. A tree doesn't *try* to grow, it just grows. A flower doesn't *try* to open, it just opens. Don't try; *do*.

You never hear real power players say, "I'm trying." They say, "I am doing." Oprah didn't say she was going to *try* to start a network. She just started it. You either do things or you don't. The security blanket that *trying* gives us is false, stagnant, and dangerous.

I'm not suggesting laziness—just the opposite, in fact. Work is important and necessary. Take inspired action on your desires to accomplish and to *do* every single day. No one wants to pay to watch you do something with *effort,* but everyone will want to see you do your work with a sense of ease, confidence, and self-assuredness. We want to move into a space of working because we love the work and love creating for the sake of creating. We do the work so that we afford ourselves the luxury of effortlessness. This holds true for your new practice as well. You do the work of scheduling it, you do the work of bravely moving through the discomfort of the emotional detox, you do the work of getting your buns in the chair twice a day every day. If you do that, you afford yourself the luxury of effortlessness when you're in the sitting itself.

As you continue your twice-daily practice, you'll cultivate confidence in your brain's ability to perceive and execute based on your own observations, insights, education, preparation, and experience. You have everything you need to actually make something happen. Most of us have spent a long time strengthening the "trying" muscle because it gives us an easy way out if we don't succeed. Get rid of that safety net. Go out and *do* with elegance and confidence. You might "fail." Do it anyway.

Once you break the apology addiction and the trying trap, you can step into the most amazing version of you. Ideally, we work passionately on the task at hand and do the best that we can with our current abilities and understanding. How do we find peace with such a bold shift in habits? Step 1: Scheduling and committing to your new twice-a-day habit. This will allow you to cultivate a level of ease that comes from trusting yourself and your ever-increasing cognitive capabilities.

Eyes-Open Exercise

Breaking the Apology Addiction

Many of us have varying degrees of apology addiction, and it shows up in a lot of different ways, from mindlessly saying "sorry" when someone bumps into you to qualifying your work when you present it. So here's a challenge for you:

For *one whole week*, challenge yourself not to apologize. To keep track, find a special place in a journal, or even make a note in your handy smartphone, where you can keep a tally of each time you unnecessarily apologize and catch yourself after. See how many times you apologize *unnecessarily* in a week.

Pro tip: Don't turn into a nightmare person. If you've actually wronged someone, or hurt someone, or if an apology is actually relevant and needed, then by all means ask for forgiveness. What I want you to keep track of for one week is how many times you mindlessly fall into an old habit of accepting blame for something that has nothing to do with fault. Notice how your self-perception changes when you stop engaging in this behavior for only a week, then decide if you want to keep the challenge going.

Ziva Case Study 6

Stress Less, Accomplish More

CHRISTIE ORROS, REALTOR

I started Ziva because I heard Emily had a highly sought-after practice aimed toward high achievers. I thought this might be exactly what I needed to learn, and who I needed to learn it from.

What I wanted was relief from stress, anxiety, and mild depression induced partly by heredity and partly by the daily trappings of being a full-time Realtor. Pre-Ziva, I was working about sixty to seventy hours a week, depending on the season. I was burned out, to say the least. When you feel chained to work all day, every day, it affects your entire life: You start to find social events an annoyance because they are taking you away from time that could be spent working; you take your stress out on those who you know will stick around; depression comes along when you use adrenaline to keep your head above the workload; you quit doing anything not work-production related; on rare days off, you find yourself staying in bed, half awake, for twelve-plus hours straight, attempting to "recharge" in some way.

So . . . yeah, I needed some help.

I spent three years on a mild antidepressant and decided that masking the symptoms wasn't solving it for me. I needed to go inward and change something. Off the pills, on to the meditation.

I took the Ziva course and have been meditating twice a day for more than two years now.

Emily has this saying: "Stress less . . . accomplish more." As a skeptic, I thought, *Seriously? Come on! I am loving this Mindfulness, Meditation, and Manifesting thing, but that may be taking it a bit too far.* Seven months later, at the height of the busy season in Florida real estate sales, I found myself working only forty to forty-five hours a week. At first I panicked, thinking, *Am I failing as a Realtor? Why am I not working constantly? I heard from another Realtor; she worked twenty hours this weekend but I only worked six. Am I going to go hungry next month and lose everything because I'm not working as much as she is?* Then I looked at my production numbers—and I actually had to check them twice because I didn't believe what I was seeing! I actually sold *more* real estate in the first six months of this year of meditation than I did the entire previous year without taking fifteen precious minutes twice a day out of my packed schedule. That's right—I worked less . . . and accomplished more. I also realized that I was sleeping better and had not felt the dark cloud of depression following me for months. I even found myself listening more and talking less.

Your changes may be similar or quite different, but I promise you that you will find the process worth the investment on many levels. I cannot recommend this practice enough.

Ziva Case Study 7

From Good to Great

ARI WHITTEN, BESTSELLING AUTHOR, DAD, AND HEALTH COACH

My life was far from a mess when I started Ziva. In fact, life was already pretty damn good. I had a thriving business, a wonderful partner, and a beautiful one-year-old son.

Yet not all was perfect. With the demands of running a business and the seven-day-workweek life of an entrepreneur, plus being a new dad, life certainly was hectic at times. So much to do, constant interruptions—add sleep deprivation from a baby into the mix, and it became tough to get things done. As projects started to pile up, it got to the point where I was chronically feeling overwhelmed, always feeling like there was more to do than I had time for. My mind was constantly preoccupied, trying to keep track of everything I needed to do. That led to low-level stress and anxiety permeating my days. It became harder to get stuff done and find the motivation to do work, and I wasn't able to relax and simply enjoy downtime with my family or really be in the moment when surfing or rock climbing. My sleep was disturbed because I couldn't turn my mind off at night. My body was in a constant state of tension, including aches and pains due to stress. It started to sap my energy and impair cognitive performance, motivation, and physical performance during sports. It became a vicious cycle.

At some point during this cycle, I became conscious of the fact that I was losing the ability to be present and relaxed—to just laugh, play, and enjoy the moment. So I made the decision that it was time to start meditating again.

I say "again" because I had dabbled in many types of esoteric meditation years prior to starting my business, but nothing ever really stuck with me or became a daily practice.

Then I stumbled across Emily at a conference. She guided the whole group through a meditation, and I thought, *Damn, this woman is great! I want to learn her style of meditation!*

I made the decision to take her course about eight months ago, and I'm so glad I did.

What I've experienced is a profound relaxation, where everything calms down, and instead of all that tension and anxiety building up through the course of the day and then feeling wiped out, now I feel relaxed and refreshed all day long.

None of the demands on me changed in any way. The thing that changed is my brain, and my ability to handle those demands.

It is possible to go through life and do what you need to do while being stressed, low energy, lacking motivation, anxious, in a crappy mood, and not performing well mentally or physically. But you could do all the same things you need to do each day from a place of relaxation, serenity, joy, and even playfulness.

I spent years in the former state. Now—thanks to Ziva—I am squarely in the latter state, and I feel great!

All this because of these two little blocks of the 3 M's. It's like wiping the whiteboard clean twice a day. As soon as you do that, you go back into this beautiful place of relaxation.

I am getting more done than ever, I am present and relaxed with my family, my sleep is phenomenal, my surfing and climbing have never been better (I've never been more fearless or performed as well as I do now), and, most important, I am smiling and laughing while going through my day.

This practice has truly changed my brain, and if we had done before-and-after MRI scans, I have no doubt that would be verified. This is a practice I am committed to doing every day for the rest of my life.

FROM OM TO OMG!

ONCE PEOPLE GET OVER THE MISPERCEPTION THAT THEY should magically be able to "clear their minds" during meditation, they start to believe that if they have thoughts, they should only be pure thoughts of enlightenment and bliss. Ironically, this mind-set often keeps folks from talking about one of the biggest benefits of meditation: better sex. In fact, this chapter may be the number one reason you picked up this book. If that's the case, I'd like to open by saying, *You're welcome.*

Now, at first glance, it may seem a little out of place to have a chapter on how meditation makes you better in bed in a book that is designed for high achievers—after all, this is not exactly the sort of thing that will typically help you get ink on a contract. But have you ever felt as if your sex life was in something of a rut? If so, it kind of makes everything in life a little duller, doesn't it? On the other hand, the morning after you rocked your partner's world (and maybe even had your own mind blown in the process), you walk around with a little extra swagger and a little more confidence that you could do anything, didn't you? That's what I'm talking about. Up-leveling your performance in the bedroom, besides being a pretty fantastic benefit in and of itself, can also help you up-level your performance in the boardroom. (Besides, we high achievers tend to be a little competitive and want to feel safe in the knowledge that we are the best at *everything*.) As the saying goes, how you do anything is how you do everything. So let's talk specifically about how the 3 M's can up-level your performance in the bedroom.

Mind-blowing sex may seem like an unlikely benefit of meditation, but the Z Technique can actually do much more for you in the bedroom than Viagra. For too long, meditation has been associated with asceticism and monks, which is why it's taken us so long to get around to exploring its effects on sex (just in case you needed one more reminder that this practice is definitely *not* for monks).

» First, the Obvious . . .

A student of mine who is a lawyer in New York City came to Ziva because he was dealing with anxiety. He joined a group meditation one year after he started with Ziva and said, "You joked once before about meditation making my sex better, but what's happening for me is crazy. It feels un-meditate-y to say, but my sex life is stunning now." *Animalistic, raw,* and *mind-blowing* were the most memorable adjectives he used to describe his newfound sexual prowess. He told me that since the first week of taking the course, he noticed not only that he was able to last much longer during intercourse, but also that he felt more control over his orgasms and had much more energy, and a stronger sex drive as a result.

Another student vouched for the fact that, after only one week of being fully committed to a regular, twice-a-day practice, she had an orgasm *every single time* she and her partner had adult playtime—a fact that had definitely not been true before she came to Ziva.

Obviously meditation was not the only contributing factor in these scenarios—after all, it takes two to tango—but based on what we regularly hear from Ziva graduates, these experiences are not at all uncommon.

So why do the 3 M's make you better in bed? Well, let's consider context first. Many of us are stressed out, whether from work, our relationships, money, or any of our many responsibilities. We're often so caught up in our heads that we're not fully in touch with our bodies. We're also frequently so busy reviewing the past and rehearsing the future that we're not present in the right now. None of these things are ingredients for a great sex life. And on top of everything else, increased levels of cortisol and adrenaline from stress decrease both sexual desire and sexual performance. Sexual trauma can also play a role here. Remember: We shouldn't be asking how meditation can do so much good, but how stress can mess up so many things.

But there are a few other reasons, besides the basic biology of stress release, that help make these mental techniques such powerful tools for improving your sexual performance.

» 1. Deep body rest, which means more energy for sex.

How many times has being "too tired" been your excuse for not having sex? You're not alone: Exhaustion is one of the most common reasons couples don't have as much sex as they would like. According to a recent study by the National Sleep Foundation, about one in every four married or cohabitating American couples claim they're so sleep deprived that they're often too fatigued to have sex.[1] It's pretty hard to feel turned on if you're exhausted, and unfortunately, many of us feel so worn out after a busy day that the last thing on our minds is having a high-energy romp in the bedroom.

But remember that when you meditate, you de-excite the nervous system and give your body rest that is deeper than sleep; as a result, you actually feel more awake afterward. This jolt of energy may be just what you need after work to energize you for a passionate evening with your partner. No more "I have a headache" excuses. When you're more rested, you feel better, and when you feel good, your body is far more likely to be ready, willing, and able to perform when you want it to. (*Bonus feature:* If migraines have been keeping you from getting busy, we have a 90 percent success rate with migraines at Ziva.)

» 2. The 3 M's decrease stress, which means better performance.

Your new habit can help with so much more than just getting in the mood beforehand; it can help you *during* sex, too. Mindfulness strengthens the mind-body connection, making you more aware of your body and the moment-to-moment physical sensations running through it. When you're experiencing the world through all five of your senses as opposed to just through your brain, you're more receptive to every sensation—which is obviously pretty helpful when you're having sex. This is another great reason to make sure you are already scheduling and committing to your daily Z Technique time, especially the first M: mindfulness. The Come to Your Senses exercise will help with this.

The act of de-exciting the nervous system also helps relax your brain and body, which makes it easier for you to become aroused. There's a reason that almost every civilization since the beginning of time has had some sort of mating ritual; things like a nice dinner, champagne, oysters, chocolate, and music can help set the mood and relax you for sex. The more relaxed you are going into the act itself, the more likely you are to enjoy it and therefore the more likely you are to climax.

This is serious business—increased cortisol levels can prevent female orgasm entirely! According to a recent study, women whose cortisol levels exceed a certain amount can become physically incapable of orgasm.[2] Think about it: Do you feel aroused when you're stressed out? Probably not. And men are not off the hook. According to Nelson E. Bennett, M.D., an erectile dysfunction expert at the Lahey Clinic, "Stress, fear, anxiety, worry, and frustration cause your body to release adrenaline, which constricts your blood vessels, and that is bad for getting a good erection."[3]

Meditation moves you out of fight or flight and into stay and play. Within a few days of starting a meditation practice, adrenaline and cortisol levels drop throughout the body. The meditation combined with mindfulness and manifesting will help your brain naturally begin producing more of those wonderful bliss chemicals, dopamine and serotonin, even during the hours of the day when you aren't in the chair. This bliss chemistry sticks around in the body and helps to increase your sexual appetite and even increase the intensity of orgasm.[4]

Meditation also helps strengthen your sense of connectedness to your partner—or feeling connected to your own body if you're enjoying some "me time." Instead of being distracted about what happened at work today or your to-do list for tomorrow, you're better able to stay in the right here, right now. Additionally, meditation increases mirror neuron functioning, meaning you're more likely to be highly attuned to what your partner is feeling (more on that in a bit). This fact, coupled with the fact that you're relaxed and present, gives you the potential to be a far more intuitive and generous lover.

» 3. Less distracted, more present.

Most of us have an overdeveloped left brain, and as you know, the left brain's job is to review the past and rehearse the future. This can keep us trapped in a past/future thought cycle and rob us of the ability to be fully present in the right now, which is the only time an orgasm can happen.

The right brain is in charge of present moment awareness, and this is the part of the brain that meditation takes to the gym. The longer we have a daily practice, the more cohesion and neuroplasticity we create, which balance the right and left hemispheres of the brain. The result of this is an increase in attention, awareness, and computing power for the task at hand . . . and depending on what you're into, it may take quite a few hands! Nobody likes a distracted lover. The experience is better for everyone when you're fully committed to the moment.

» 4. Stop looking to your partner to complete you.

"You complete me" is probably the most damaging phrase to come out of Hollywood. No one can complete you. As we learned from the chapter on the "I'll be happy when . . ." syndrome, no partner, job, degree, or number of zeros in your bank account can complete you. Your new Z Technique is going to contribute to your sex life in that it helps you access fulfillment internally, which is the not-so-obvious key to a successful relationship with another person. Meditation gives you a means to access the happiness inside you, making you less likely to look to or for a partner to complete you. (Besides, when is neediness ever attractive?) When you're able to access your own fulfillment and bliss internally, you're able to show up 100 percent in a relationship, making you a better partner. If you're 80 percent fulfilled, the relationship will be a place to *deliver* that fulfillment, not somewhere you go to get the missing 20 percent. Imagine how much more enjoyable it would be if your relationship was an outlet for your fulfillment versus a place to try (and fail) to fill yourself up?

» 5. Your partner might think you're psychic.

If you haven't heard about mirror neurons yet, get ready. Scientists say that mirror neurons are going to do for psychology what unlocking the mystery of DNA did for biology.[5] Think of mirror neurons as tiny boomerangs emitted from your brain that go and dance with your lover's mirror neurons and then report back. Mirror neurons allow you to "intuit" what your partner is feeling. They are why you cringe if you watch someone getting hurt and smile back automatically when someone smiles at you. Mirror neurons are one of the reasons porn is a multibillion-dollar industry; simply watching someone else being pleasured can create pleasure in your brain. They are, essentially, the biological basis for empathy.

Get this: As meditation develops new synapses and neural pathways in the brain, it also increases mirror neuron functioning. This helps you to receive more pleasure from seeing your partner have pleasure, which will make you a far more intuitive and generous partner.

» Meditation as Foreplay

Here's the icing on top of all this sexy cake: You can incorporate elements of the Z Technique into your pre-sex routine to help you, in real time, get away from overthinking about the reports that are due tomorrow or worrying that all your bits and pieces aren't as perfect as you'd like them to be, and get in the best possible headspace (which is, basically, no headspace at all).

Remember the Come to Your Senses exercise you learned as the mindfulness element of the Z Technique? Well, here's another place you can use this tool to pull yourself decidedly into the present moment.

Either in the shower, before a rendezvous, or as you prepare your space, simply take a few deep belly breaths and walk yourself through each of your senses: hearing, feeling, seeing, tasting, and smelling, then all five at the same time. Really giving yourself full permission to be so deliciously human, so incredibly present in your body. The more you practice this ritual, the more natural it will become, and the easier it will be to perform while you're brushing your teeth, folding back the covers, and putting on—or taking off—your sexiest lingerie. Really good sex, after all, calls upon all your senses. (That's what being "sensual" means, after all—engaging the senses in a heightened manner.) By the time you reach the end of this quick roll call and are holding all your senses simultaneously in one awareness, you'll be so deeply in the moment that your logical left brain will be ready to sit down, shut up, and buckle in for a wild ride.

» Creative Energy and Sexual Energy

Okay, Emily: I definitely love the sex tips and all, but I picked up this book to help me up-level my career. I hear you, buzzkill. Fine, let's bring this conversation back to the extremely practical side of things—namely, how your new and improved sexual empowerment will help you reach new heights of creativity and innovation in the boardroom as well as the bedroom.

Have you ever stopped to think why Taylor Swift, Adele, and virtually every country star have built careers on writing songs after heartbreak? It's because creative energy and sexual energy are essentially the same thing. Have you ever started working out after a breakup? Did you ever write a poem or take a painting class after heartbreak? Sexual/Creative energy needs an outlet, and when a relationship ends, that sexual energy can start to manifest in other ways, whether it's writing songs, writing poetry, or repainting your room. It is important to be aware of this because if you don't turn that unused sexual energy into something creative, it can become destructive (e.g., the weeklong bender, the Netflix binge, or maxing out your credit cards shopping online).

It is true, of course, that sex can harness some of that creative energy, which may seem like a disadvantage when you're looking to increase your innovation at work—at least at first. But consider the fact that increased sexual performance actually creates more sexual energy (we want to keep doing what we're good at, right?). This means that an up-leveling in our sex lives can lead to an up-leveling in our professional productivity. I say this with a word of caution, however; sexual and creative energy are resources, a kind of energetic currency, if you will, and it is wise to be conscious of how you're choosing to use them. It's not advisable to dedicate 100 percent of this intense energy to sex, just as it's not healthy to channel it 100 percent into work. ("All work and no play makes Jack a dull boy," right?) You should be sure you're expending that capital in the ways that best serve your current priorities.

The good news, however, is that they are renewable resources—ones that can come back stronger each time they are exhausted and replenished. When you feel that you're thriving sexually in a reciprocal relationship, your confidence in your other abilities will increase. Conversely, when your career performance is surging forward, you'll likely feel more energized in all areas of your life, including your sexuality. After all, very little puts you in the mood to "celebrate" as much as a major success, contract, or promotion. Find harmony between work and play that helps feed the cycle of confidence and empowerment, and reap the rewards!

The most important link between mindfulness and really good sex is that the former makes us more present—which means you can enjoy each micro-moment, rather than looking at sex as an outcome-oriented task. As you continue to take your brain to the gym, specifically by strengthening your right brain, you'll find the beautiful benefits of being fully in the present begin to fill every corner of your life . . . including the bedroom.

Being present does not mean you live entirely in the moment at all times at the expense of your responsibilities; it simply means you no longer allow stress to dictate your life or define your experiences—not your career, not your personal goals, not your relationships, not your sex.

Think of the sexiest person you can. What attributes come to mind? Do they exude confidence, intelligence, and humor? Do they wear their body well (whatever that means to you)? Do they make you feel like you're the only person on the planet when they talk to you?

You know who you probably didn't include on that list? Someone who is freaking out, frazzled, messy, slouchy, down on themselves, sallow, or sick-looking. *Stress isn't sexy,* and neither are its effects on our brains and our bodies. But someone whose mind is dynamic and whose body is healthy—whether that is through sharp, chiseled muscles or soft, inviting curves or some delicious middle ground—embodies the things we are biologically hardwired to find attractive in a mate.

Conversely, health, wit, and self-assuredness are all generally the traits we would all wish for ourselves, too. We are always better lovers when we are feeling confident and sexy ourselves. Do you want to be thought of as attractive and engaging? Vibrant and vigorous? Adopt a practice that will allow you to move away from whatever is detrimental to your physical and psychological wellness, and toward your best self. That's what this practice can do for you. *That's* sexy. It makes you want to close your eyes and dive in, doesn't it?

Ziva Case Study 8

A First Time for Everything

ANONYMOUS

I like to think of myself as being in touch with myself on a sexual level and had never been one to be afraid of voicing my needs to a partner. That said, I was pretty frustrated that for the first six years of my life as a sexually active adult, I had never been able to achieve an orgasm just from intercourse. Not even close. Since I had a fulfilling (or so I thought) sex life outside of this, I chalked it up to being "just one of those women" for whom it wouldn't happen. I had many friends who were similar, so I pretty much gave up on internal orgasm being a possibility. Writing that now makes me cringe.

Later, when I took my Ziva course, I didn't pay much attention when Emily discussed the potential sexual benefits. I thought about it much more as a stress reliever/cognitive performance thing for me, not realizing that *it's all connected*. I thought at most it meant stronger, more pleasurable orgasms—not necessarily more of them or a different kind. I also wasn't seeing anyone at the time, so this wasn't top of mind for me. (I was, however, a basket case at work. Go figure.)

A few months into my practice, I started seeing someone and noticed almost immediately that my external orgasms were much stronger, despite a fairly predictable experience otherwise. Then one day, in the middle of having sex, I was completely caught off guard and had an orgasm! I stopped what I was doing immediately and said, "Well . . . that was weird," and explained to him that it was the first time that ever happened for me. It was an ego boost for him, even if I knew the real reason behind it!

Since that time, having an orgasm exclusively from internal stimulation is a much more frequent occurrence. I've noticed, too, that the times when I'm not as regular with my daily practice, they become more elusive. It's become one of the primary motivators for keeping honest with my two-times-a-day sitting (who doesn't want more orgasms?), since I can almost always count on it happening for me if I am at my most relaxed and present.

This has been a huge selling point for meditation for my friends as well. Once I told my friends who thought they were also "just those women" for whom it wouldn't happen, they all started to believe my hype. I even got one to take the zivaONLINE course, and when Emily asked in the online community why she was there, she answered, "I'm here for the orgasms!"

Eyes-Open Exercise

Heart to Heart

This exercise is about establishing a bond with your partner, creating that sense of generosity and openness that inevitably leads to heightened intimacy and connection. This exercise might be out of the norm for most couples, so I recommend asking first. You could try something like, "Hey, do you want to try something new that might enhance our sex life?" If your partner agrees, then follow the steps below.

1. Face your partner, place your right hand on their heart, and have them do the same with their right hand over your heart.
2. Both of you place your left hand on top of your heart, and look into each other's eyes. It may (read: probably will) be uncomfortable, but continue to hold eye contact even through the laughter and nervousness that arises. Once that passes (I promise it will), ask your partner to say their biggest dream or goal. Then you share yours.
3. Now spend 2 to 3 minutes imagining this dream of your partner's as if it is happening now. Imagine them stepping into their full potential, the confidence and sexiness that comes with that. Manifesting is powerful work to do on yourself, and it's even more powerful to do for someone else.

4. Imagine harnessing all the energy of this dream and give it to your partner like a gift. Take a deep inhale, and as you exhale, imagine your breath filling them with the energy of this dream, as well as blasting them with love. Now switch roles and then be open to receive what they are giving to you. Let it be a cycle, enjoying the give and the take. You are keeping eye contact this whole time. If possible, favor your partner's left eye and have them do the same with yours.

5. After 2 to 3 minutes, or when it feels like things have come to a natural conclusion, thank your partner, hug it out if you feel inspired to, and let things progress as they will with this new, profound sense of intimacy and generosity.

For a guided visualization for better sex, head to www .zivameditation.com/bookbonus.

» 12 «

MIND THE GAP

A FEW MONTHS AFTER TAKING THE COURSE, A STUDENT NAMED Warren found himself on the subway, trying to get to the airport for a flight, with all his luggage. And I'm not talking about a cute carry-on. I'm talking three full-size juggernauts, one carry-on, and a duffel bag. It was a feat of superhuman strength that he was able to get these bags through any of the subway turnstiles, but he had made it all the way to the airport tram when he suddenly found himself not only with an unreasonable amount of luggage, but also a MetroCard that wouldn't scan. As he stood at the turnstile, fruitlessly sliding his card again and again with a line of impatient commuters twenty people deep lining up behind him, he had the sinking realization that his card was out of money and he was running out of time before his flight took off. The only way to refill the card was to get to the MetroCard machines at the other end of the station, which would require dragging his suitcases while cutting across a line of ten turnstiles, each with its own line of people trying to swipe through. In short, this was a travel nightmare.

Though Warren's self-admitted old habitual reaction would have been to curse up a storm, kick the machine, or scream in frustration, this time he took a breath and actually laughed at the hilarity of it all. He then stepped to the side and moved his luggage as best he could to let others pass while he tried to calmly figure out the best strategy to cross the crowded station. It was a simple, almost involuntary act of surrender, but it made a massive difference in the way the rest of the day played out.

Before Warren even had time to think of a way to traverse the station, a man behind him saw the pickle he was in and kindly asked, "Hey—can I swipe you through?" And with a quick motion, he ran his card through the reader to open the gate to allow Warren and his luggage to pass.

Warren recalled later how amazed he had been not only by his own very different and very calm response to a situation that, before he was a regular meditator, would have instantly sapped a day's worth of adaptation energy and potentially led to a missed flight and thousands of dollars in tickets, hotels, and hassles; he was also struck by the kind response from the stranger who gladly shared a swipe of his card to help him out of a tricky spot. "I don't think he would have done that if I had been yelling or acting angry," he said. "Because *I* was calm, *he* felt willing to help."

The gap you have between stimulus and reaction—that split second that less stress affords you to choose how you'll respond to a given situation—can affect the direction of your entire day as well as the days of the people around you. It can even affect your reputation and effectiveness as a leader. Your ability to pause, consider, and intentionally *choose* your response, rather than being launched involuntarily into fight-or-flight mode, is a direct reflection of your own resilience and your ability to lead. With every high-demand situation you're faced with, you'll now have a choice. Are you going to choose victimhood or mastery?

RESILIENCE: The capacity to recover quickly from difficulties. The more resilient you are, the more freedom you have to choose how you want to respond to the hand you're dealt.

» Martyr or Master?

Does the martyr role come easily for you? I don't mean to blame or shame anyone with that question. If so, here's some good news: You can only be a martyr if you're dealing with limited resources. And now that you're going to have a twice-daily practice of tapping into the very source of energy, you'll no longer have limited resources. When we feel like a martyr or get stressed, we're not *choosing* to launch into fight or flight; it's an involuntary body reaction that we inherited from many millennia spent fighting tigers. Now that most of our demands are things other than predatory attacks and we're cultivating the daily habit of stressing less and tapping the source of creativity, we're earning the freedom to choose how we respond to demands.

I'm not suggesting you'll never get stressed—sometimes that's the most appropriate reaction, and could keep you alive. Remember, it's not bad for you to *get* stressed, but it is terrible for you to *stay* stressed. What's going to change after a few months of regular practice is you'll start to have the power to choose how you want to respond to demands—is fight or flight actually relevant in a scenario or would you rather step into the new now and interact with your circumstances in a different manner. This is where the daily discipline comes into play as you commit to managing your stress instead of letting it manage you.

When you move through the 3 M's twice a day, you're training yourself to access your right brain's intuition and present moment awareness as the default. As you strengthen this side of your brain to bring it more in line with the development of your left brain, you'll likely find yourself responding to high-demand situations in a far calmer and more deliberate way. The reason is quite simple: When you have the ability to be truly present in each moment during situations that are particularly high demand, then you can more easily see the most relevant action to take now . . . and now . . . and now. Your mind is not already racing eight steps ahead to one of five different potential outcomes, nor is it consumed by what it should have done differently leading up to this moment of panic; you simply recognize the situation for what it is, surrender your illusion of control, and look for the next best step to take to resolve it. There is a time and a place for strategic thinking, of course, but only after the immediate circumstances have been evaluated and your body's fight-or-flight mechanism either engaged or shut down. This is the way we avoid a dozen tiny victimhoods each day, where we blame other people and blame circumstances rather than choosing to take responsibility and strengthen our resiliency.

Consider this scenario: You're driving to work and someone tries to cut you off, which makes your stress hormones start pumping. You have a couple of options:

> You can take a moment, a breath, a gap, and recognize that you are not in actual mortal peril at this moment. This leads you to turn off your automatically triggered fight-or-flight response and simply allow that car to pass you by; or

> You can honk your horn, flip off the other driver, which leads to their own fight-or-flight response getting activated so that they speed up, get right on your tail, and tap your bumper. You manage to swerve and get way ahead of them, but in gunning it you miss the fact that you're flying past a cop at

55 mph in a 35 mph zone, and the next thing you know, the original guy speeds past you, laughing and pointing, as you're pulled over on the side of the road getting a ticket.

How much did that one (seemingly small) moment cost you, either in time, repairs, court fees, or sheer embarrassment? Was reacting with a stress-based response by flipping off that person really worth it in the long run? And even if you don't end up with a dented bumper or points on your license, did giving that person the bird really solve anything? In retrospect, would you have been better served by keeping both hands on the wheel, your eyes on the road, and your mind attuned to the speed traps ahead, or, better yet, simply enjoying the interesting podcast playing on your car stereo?

Here's the thing. We all know how we *should* act: eat more vegetables, exercise every day, go to bed before midnight, and call your mom more often. It's not that hard . . . yet most of us aren't doing it. Why? Because we don't act in accordance with what we know; we act in accordance with the baseline level of stress in our nervous systems.

I'm not telling you anything new, nor do I have any interest in telling you how to act. I am simply encouraging you to develop a daily discipline to help you act more in accordance with what you already know to be true. That's what meditation does: It rids you of the stress that clouds your mind and taxes your body. It allows you easier access to the ideal self that already exists within you. Remember, meditation is like a hardware upgrade for your brain so that you can run whatever software you already have in place—Christianity, Judaism, Islam, Buddhism, Hinduism can all run more effectively on an optimized brain machine. No wonder meditation is practiced by so many of the top achievers across so many different industries and faiths.

» The Natural Leader

Think for a minute about the worst boss with whom you've ever worked. Now think about the best. Chances are, no matter what your field, the differences came down to the level of mastery that person had over himself or herself. A leader who is chronically stressed, unpredictable, disorganized, unmotivated, uninspired and uninspiring, flies off the handle, blames other people, or just seems like a loose cannon is someone who probably lets circumstances dictate their performance and is not actually a leader at all, no matter what their job title. On the other hand, a leader who is calm, self-possessed, maintains composure under pressure, thinks clearly even when demands are pressing, has keen instincts, and seems to have a healthy relationship with stress is someone whom you trust to have your back and to act with the best interest of the team in mind.

Which kind of person do other people want to follow, hire, partner with, collaborate with, elect, or marry? More important, which kind of person do you want to be?

In the documentary *Jim & Andy*, about Jim Carrey's immersive work to play comedian Andy Kaufman in the film *Man on the Moon*, Carrey talked about his early days as a stand-up comedian. He initially tried to do a routine that involved a lot of give-and-take with the audience, and he found himself bombing night after night. He would start the set with banter, asking people about themselves or about their day, and he needed them to be engaged for his act to move forward, which made the audience feel like part of the weight of the show was on their shoulders. Finally, one night, Jim asked the same questions but didn't rely on the audience to fill the empty space; instead of waiting for a response, he answered his own question with his soon-to-be catchphrase: "Aaaaalllllriighty then!" The audience broke into hysterics. He realized in that moment that his role as the entertainer was not to put other people on the spot by making them feel they had to perform themselves, but to make them feel absolved of responsibility. His job was to let the audience know he was in charge. As soon as he took that responsibility onto himself, the audience was able to relax and enjoy the show. No matter how you feel about Jim Carrey's comedy, the lesson is an important one: Leaders become far more effective and win over the rest of the team when they radiate a sense of self-mastery in any scenario, which allows everyone around them to feel more at ease.

While I think we can all agree that a control freak or someone who speaks only in monologues without getting input from others is probably not a good leader, the underlying idea here is sound. When you assume your role with confidence and self-mastery, handling changes in expectations in stride, people will naturally gravitate toward you because that confidence you exude in turn gives them the comfort to relax into their own roles around you. In Nature, the alpha dog of a pack asserts leadership by his or her presence more so than any show of force, so good dog trainers advise humans trying to establish a healthy relationship with their dog to use the same strategy. There is an automatic gravitation toward someone whose energy is calm and confident, especially in the midst of uncertain or chaotic situations. Whatever your role is—CEO, parent, teacher, manager, supervisor—when you enter your sphere of influence with a mind-set of mastery rather than victimhood, you're putting out a vibe to everyone around you as to what kind of a person you are and what kind of a leader you can be.

When you use the Z Technique, twice a day for fifteen minutes at a time, *you're honing your body's ability to adapt its automatic stress response to an appropriate level for the actual circumstances you're facing*. By making that internal source of bliss and fulfillment more easily accessible, your practice begins to reprogram your brain to be more disciplined and intentional with how you handle every situation throughout your day. Remember, surrender is *not* about giving up, but about trusting that a higher power is at work and that you can rely on your intuition to help you navigate rather than manipulate your environment. If you find yourself struggling, take a moment to reframe your perspective with that question we discussed earlier. Instead of "Why is this happening *to* me?" ask yourself "Why is this happening *for* me?" By taking just a moment to flip the script, you're taking the power away from your reflexive responses and putting it back into your own resilience. This is how you come to recognize that you're a master, not a martyr. And when you become a master of yourself, you become empowered to perform at your highest level.

» The Least Selfish Thing You Can Do

Think back to the story that opened this chapter. When my friend Warren retained mastery of his response to the situation in the subway, someone else responded positively as well. That one interaction changed the entire trajectory of his day. He felt calmer and more surrendered, and was even able to make his upcoming flight. (And if you've traveled at all lately, you know that's no small feat!) Put yourself in his shoes for a minute: Rather than waking up late, rushing to the airport, and beginning your trip as a ball of stress, you wake up a bit early, move through the 3 M's, and flood your brain and body with dopamine and serotonin, which allows you to take that fulfillment with you on the road. Then, as the day unfolds, you respond to each situation accordingly. The gate agent, the flight attendant, your Lyft driver—they all have a positive interaction with you in the midst of a thousand neutral or negative ones. In making your day better, you've also made theirs better, which in turn affects the people with whom *they* interact.

Now think about how that positive impact compounds when you have these kinds of positive interactions day after day with the same people. When your children get the best version of you—the calm, patient you who listens and responds with intentionality rather than losing patience—they carry those feelings of security and affirmation with them to school, where they bring their best selves to the classroom and affect their teachers, who bring those good feelings home to their own family. When your partner gets the best version of you—the you who communicates openly, who loves passionately, and who projects a sense of fulfillment—they take those feelings of respect and love with them into their own workplace or environment every day and reflect them back to you at home. When your coworkers or employees or boss all get the best version of you in the workplace—the you who is innovative and creative and undaunted by challenges—they take those feelings of enthusiasm and energy about the project back to their own office or workspace, and together you motivate your team to accomplish more, which excites and inspires your customers and clients.

You stand at the center of your own sphere of influence; it's up to you what kind of energy you want to radiate outward. Yes, you get to personally enjoy the bliss and fulfillment of your own self-mastery, but you may also come to find there's a giver's high you experience as the bliss passes from person to person to person down the line. I sometimes hear from students that meditation feels selfish because they are taking a break from the day to focus entirely on themselves. My job is to help them see that this ripple effect of maintaining strength and calm in the midst of intense life circumstances can change the day of someone three, five, ten people removed from you, as everyone else is touched by your one deliberate decision to respond rather than simply to react. Their own day is made a little better by your daily commitment to yourself. Your work on healing from the effects of stress is the least selfish thing you can do, because your healing impacts every single person with whom you come into contact. *As you heal yourself, you help to heal the collective.*

Now, there are a few rare souls with whom I have come into contact during my teaching career who insist they truly do not carry stress in their bodies and do not need to heal from any long-term effects. I am not going to question their self-perception, since they obviously know themselves better than I do, but I still encourage those individuals to consider adopting a practice because of the benefits it brings to the collective. By putting in only thirty minutes a day (total), they can improve the impact they have on the people around them, which in turn affects the way those people see the world. Even if you don't think you need to stress less, you can meditate for the greater good. That is beautiful, too. Think of it as your contribution toward laundering the collective consciousness.

In fact, if it helps, think of your twice-daily practice of the Z Technique as a daily act of altruism. Sure, you get a ridiculously long list of benefits from it, but *so does everyone around you and the rest of the world*. It's hard not to see the silver lining in that.

» The Future of Self-Help

Recently, there has been a growing conversation in many self-help circles that the whole concept of "self-help" is going away, being replaced instead by the idea of helping the collective. I can't think of a more beautiful direction for us to be trending as a community, nor of a more perfect explanation for why meditation has been making such inroads in mainstream America.

John Donne wrote back in 1624 that "No man is an island"; how much more true today, when technology connects us in ways once only imagined as science fiction. Of course, many cultural commentators have pointed out that despite our interconnectedness, quite a few of us also feel more alone than ever because much of our time is spent staring at screens or living in virtual worlds. What a paradox: We are alone together and we are together in our loneliness. But no matter how connected or disconnected you feel from the rest of the world, we are still a "we." According to the Vedas, there is only one thing and we are *all* it. Our society and our world is still built on interactions, whether it's the person who makes your coffee in the morning, answers your phone call or your e-mail, or talks with you across a table or through a screen. Life is made up of relationships. Some are macro-relationships, which we have with our loved ones, our coworkers, our clients, or our students; others are micro-relationships, which last only a moment or two but can happen hundreds of times each day. The "you" you bring to each of these interactions has the tremendous potential to color everything around you. *A better you equals a better us.* When you help yourself become stronger, calmer, healthier, and more intentional, you're literally helping the collective become better. When you choose to mind the gap between reflex and action, you're ending the destructive cycle of stress, and not just for that moment but for the unquantifiable ripple effect that will follow. And that ripple effect may not be contained simply to this lifetime or this generation, either. Geneticists are starting to understand that stress and trauma can be passed down intergenerationally through epigenetic changes to the DNA. So as you heal yourself, you're not only helping to heal those around you but potentially ending cycles of trauma that have been passed down from one generation to the next. Talk about the opposite of a waste of time!

Self-help *is* social help. You are not improving in a vacuum. Your decreased stress, improved performance, enhanced intuition and innovation, and heightened sense of mastery and fulfillment are necessarily going to have spillover effects into every area of your life and the relationships that exist there. Think of it as collateral benefits of your own quest for self-improvement; or, if you prefer, think of your own up-leveling as a pretty rad side effect of your efforts to save the world. That's right—you're helping to save the world, fifteen minutes at a time.

Ziva Case Study 9

From Fight or Flight to Stay and Play

CIARAN BYRNE, ACTOR

Being born into conflict doesn't often lead to the development of inner peace. I was born during the Northern Ireland Conflict, or "the Troubles," as those of us who lived them knew them. I'm from County Down, Northern Ireland, and was born at the end of the year in which Bloody Sunday began, 1972. That decade was followed by the British and Northern Irish Recession and continued civil unrest of the 1980s; plus, I was bullied badly as a boy, so my youth was spent in literal fight or flight. It's hard to un-train your body and mind from that kind of thinking when it's all you've known for most of your formative years. I spent much of my teens and twenties either in fights or rebelling against authority figures.

Eventually, I ended up falling in love with a New Yorker and moved to Manhattan in the fall of 2008, in the midst of another recession, but now with a new wife and new family. I really loved acting; however, the economy being what it was, the opportunities to practice my art were few and far between. I had trained as a third-generation plasterer in Northern Ireland, so I began working as a drywaller to provide for my wife and daughters. I felt weighed down by years spent living in conflict. It was difficult to shake my brain's fight-or-flight reaction to every situation, which left me perpetually stressed, getting into fights more often than I want to admit and, I believe, contributing to my heart developing an electrical deficiency, which led to a quadruple ablation at age forty-two.

As I was recovering from that surgery, I heard a talk about the Ziva Technique. As I listened to Emily explain how meditation releases stress from the past, mindfulness helps you with stress in the present, and manifesting helps with your dreams for the future, I realized that this was exactly what I had been searching for without even knowing it. As a husband and a father, I needed to be the man that my daughters could see as their constant. I already had pleasure with my art and purpose with my family. But I had no peace. When faced with high-demand situations, my default was to fight. This was not the example I wanted to set. Ziva has helped me find my way to be the man I need to be for my wife and my girls. To peace. To my best life. And to the future. I am a better and more fulfilled husband, father, and artist today for two reasons. First, I work hard at being the husband, father, and artist I want to be; and secondly, I meditate twice daily, which is what I believe gives me the ability to do that work.

Northern Ireland has now found its peace (for the most part), and thanks to Ziva, a son of Northern Ireland has finally found himself on a path to peace.

Eyes-Closed Exercise

Love Bomb

Take a moment to get settled with your back supported, head free, eyes closed (after you read this, of course). Now start with the 2x Breath (see page 37 for a refresher), doubling the length of the exhale from the inhale, so inhaling for the count of 2 and exhaling for the count of 4. (As you start to build on this practice, you could actually inhale for 3 and exhale for 6.) Do this for 4 breath cycles.

Start the Love Bomb by imagining that someone you love very much is sitting about three feet in front of you. Don't worry too much about choosing the right person; usually the first person who comes to mind is the most powerful. If you can't think of anyone who inspires an intense feeling of love in you right now, you could even use your dog or cat—anything or anyone that allows you to enjoy the sensation of love.

Take a moment to imagine their face. What do their eyes look like? What does their hair look like? What are they wearing? And how does the simple fact that you're connecting change them? Are they present with you? Do they want to be seen? Are they shy? Are they hiding?

As you notice this person across from you, this person whom you love so, so much and who has brought joy to your life, allow the sensation of love to start to permeate and radiate through your entire body on the next inhale. Allow this person to wake up a feeling of love inside of you. Enjoy this wave of love and oxytocin washing through your body and, as you inhale, supercharging this feeling of love inside of you. Now, as you exhale, imagine blasting this person with as much love as you can possibly muster so that it fills every cell of their body.

Take a moment to check back in with their eyes. Did your sending them love change their eyes? Do they seem softer? Do they seem kinder? Do they feel more connected to you?

On your inhale, allow yourself to receive the love flowing back from this person, supercharging every single cell in your body with this feeling of love and gratitude. As you exhale, imagine sending that out to the entire room. Wherever you are right now, blast the whole room with love. Some people will picture this as a golden light radiating out from their body, or a white light, or even an actual wave of love.

With each inhale, you're fanning the flame of this love

sensation in the core of your body, and it gets bigger and stronger and brighter, so that it cannot be contained by the room you're in anymore and starts to spill out to the entire building—your whole house and every person in it, covered with love every time you exhale.

Now on each inhale, imagine strengthening the frequency of love in your core and on the exhale, send love to your entire city. Every person, place, and thing—all your friends, all your family, even all your enemies. I want you to blast them with love. Love is one of these beautiful resources that the more we give of it, the more we receive.

On your next breath, breathing that sensation into your body and then letting it spill out, let it radiate out to your entire country. All the different political parties, all the different religions, all the different races, sending them all as much love as you possibly can—everyone in your whole country.

If you seem to be losing that sensation of love internally, come back to that one person whom you love very much, and imagine seeing their face as they sit a few feet from you, and let that rekindle the sensation of love internally.

Now imagine wrapping the entire planet with this beautiful feeling of love. This might sound a little cheesy or hippie-dippie, but really, truly, the only antidote to fear is love. You cannot fight fear with fear; we can only do that with love. So as we inhale, we supercharge every cell in our body with love, and then we blast that out to the entire planet Earth, letting it create a space of unity and connection. Imagine that, for just a moment, someone you know or someone you love, or even a stranger, can actually feel this love that you're sending, that you're allowing to navigate the globe. Maybe someone's feeling a little down or all alone; maybe now they start to smile or somehow feel less alone.

On your next breath, breathing in and feeling the sensation of love in every single cell in your body from the top of your head to the bottom of your toes, send that love to the entire universe as you exhale. Beyond the solar system, beyond the galaxies, beyond the clusters of galaxies, and out into the entirety of all that is—allowing your imagination to expand as far as it can conceive, reminding yourself that you are a part of the universe, and the universe is a part of you.

According to the Vedas, there's only one thing, and we're all it. Think about that for a moment. *There's only one thing, and we're all it.* This means that the exact same matter and energy that makes up every star, in every galaxy in the entire universe, is the exact same matter and energy that makes up every cell in your body. So take a moment to surrender into that sense of expansiveness and connectedness, and know that as you blast the entire universe with love, it's simultaneously sending it back to you.

Now, from this space of expansiveness, surrender, and connectedness, start to bring your awareness back into your whole body. Allow yourself to undulate between an awareness of the whole body and the whole universe, playing with the simultaneity of individuality and totality, of left brain and right brain, of body and universe, imagining for a moment that you are one wave on a giant ocean of consciousness. The wave is a part of the ocean, and the ocean is a part of the wave.

Set your intention to take this feeling with you throughout the rest of the day. If you start to get frustrated or angry with someone, come back to this and remind yourself, *I already sent you love today, so I can tap back into this even when things start to get frustrating or overwhelming*. Taking a delicious, deep inhale, wake up your body, move your hands, move your feet, and, in your own time, start to slowly, gently open your eyes.

It's kind of fun, right? Blasting the whole planet with love. I find that it really helps in situations of conflict. If I start to get angry with a taxi driver, or someone behind the counter, I remember, *You know what? I already sent this person love today. They actually are a part of me, and I am a part of them*. It's a nice way to come back to a sense of connection. If you would like to sit back, relax, and enjoy me leading you through the Love Bomb, you can listen here: www.zivameditation.com/bookbonus. You could also make a recording of you reading this exercise and listen to your own voice guiding you through.

» 13 «

UP-LEVEL YOUR PERFORMANCE

IT IS MY SINCEREST HOPE THAT YOU FEEL EXCITED AND EM-
powered by what you've read so far and by your decision to embark
on this journey of stressing less and accomplishing more.

I know there's a stereotype that meditators are just "bliss bun-
nies" who float around on clouds and talk in artificially soothing
tones. Are there some people like that? Sure. But now that meditation is moving into the mainstream, there are far more pragmatists
who have embraced the practice and who still act and sound like
normal people, who don't speak in "yoga voice" and have the ability
to *not* turn everything into a ceremony—they just do life far more
efficiently and effectively than before. Meditation doesn't turn you
into a sedate, passive person; just look at all the examples we've seen
from many of the world's top performers—some of whom I've had
the honor of teaching—who have experienced exactly the opposite!
What it really does is allow you to access and enhance the very best
parts of who you are—and who you want to be. It doesn't change you;
it makes you more yourself, but the best version of you rather than
the sick, sad, and stressed you. Because the Z Technique focuses on
three distinct practices for a multifaceted mental experience, it helps
you be fully in the present (mindfulness), heal from the past (meditation), and consciously create your future (manifesting). It offers a

complete overhaul of whatever aspects of your life, experiences, and ambitions need up-leveling.

Let's take a hot second to reflect on the incredible benefits and advantages a twice-daily practice can bring:

> If this offered nothing more than a reduction of stress stored in your body and an increased ability to elegantly handle daily demands, wouldn't that be worth it? Once you commit to a twice-a-day practice, you open yourself up to countless new opportunities that stress may have been blocking without you even knowing about them.

> If this offered nothing more than a better night's sleep, wouldn't it be worth it? If you entered every day with a fresh mind and more energy, and only required two fifteen-minute sessions to maintain that level of energy, imagine how much more you could achieve in twenty-four hours.

> If this offered nothing more than a stronger immune system and relief from the symptoms of chronic health conditions, wouldn't it be worth it? Think about the amount of productivity you lose each year due to illnesses, aches, pains, and other physical ailments. What would you pay to drastically reduce—or even eliminate—many of those issues?

> If this offered nothing more than neuroplasticity to keep your brain young and adaptable, wouldn't it be worth it? Throw in the fact that it can also help reduce visible aging in the body (how much do you spend each year on wrinkle creams and hair dyes?) and you'd be hard-pressed to find anyone who wouldn't consider it worth the time investment.

> If this offered nothing more than rewiring your neurological pathways to make your brain better equipped to man-

age many simultaneous demands, wouldn't that be worth it? Think of the incredible value that alone adds to your role in the workplace. If two fifteen-minute sessions a day can effectively turn you into the human version of a Swiss army knife, who wouldn't want that?

> If this offered nothing more than keenly sharpened intuition, wouldn't it be worth it? Consider the amount of time you spend agonizing over choices. By empowering you to more easily recognize the subtle differences and themes in the options before you, the Z Technique can help save countless hours of internal debate—and maybe even years of regret.

> If this offered nothing more than easier access to your brain's natural flow state, wouldn't it be worth it? The ability to tap into your inherent creativity and innovation without being inhibited by self-doubt is one of the best gifts you could possibly give yourself and your career.

> And finally, if this offered nothing more than access to a sense of deep, personal fulfillment, wouldn't it be worth it? Isn't that ultimately what we're all seeking—a sense of purpose and a means of making that purpose reality?

» Making It Nonnegotiable

I realize that no matter how invaluable meditation may seem, it can still be a little intimidating at first to think about committing to something that will permanently alter your daily routine, even if just by half an hour. Remember, though, that meditation is now an essential part of your daily mental hygiene. Just as you would never leave your house without brushing your teeth (I hope), meditation will now become an equally nonnegotiable part of your routine. The way we treat and respect the nonnegotiables in our lives models for everyone else how to treat those things, too. When you fail to protect your twice-daily Z time—when you permit interruptions, answer "just a quick question" from a coworker, respond to snack requests from the kids, throw the ball for your dog—whenever you're willing to disrupt your meditation times, you're demonstrating to those around you that it's okay for them to disrupt your meditations as well. When you make it clear that this is a new nonnegotiable 2 percent fraction of your day—that you will not be pulled away from your sitting unless there are exposed bones or blood—all you are asking for is fifteen minutes to yourself twice a day—colleagues, family, and even pets will quickly learn to respect and even protect that time. If you act like those times aren't important, no one else will believe they are, either. If you prioritize them, other people will start to protect them for you. You may even start to hear your child say things like, "Mommy is a lot nicer after she meditates," or "Have you done your second meditation yet, Daddy? You seem a little cranky."

You may have seen some version of a popular lecture on how to prioritize time, illustrated with rocks, sand, and a jar. If you start by filling the jar with the sand and then pour the larger rocks on top, there is not enough room in the jar—you'll never be able to get everything inside. But if you start with the larger rocks and then pour the sand over them, letting the sand fill in the nooks and crannies, everything fits in the jar with ease. The rocks are your nonnegotiables—the major pieces of your day that need to take priority. Make the commitment to establish meditation as one of those rocks. Don't start the day with coffee, social media, or complaining; start your day for you, with something that has the sole purpose of making you better, then see how your day progresses from there. We all have the same size jar, the same number of minutes in a day; it's up to you how you choose to fill yours.

When you are first beginning your practice, one of the ways you can get used to making your Z time a priority is to strictly schedule them each day. Set an alarm on your phone to remind you to begin your sitting until it becomes habit. This not only keeps you on the wagon, but the sound can also clue in your friends, family, or coworkers that you have a nonnegotiable appointment to keep. Remember what I said about not using an alarm for Ziva? That applies to the end, not the reminder in the beginning. I still don't want you to rely on an alarm to bring you out, but I absolutely *do* want you to set an alarm as a reminder to dive into your new twice-a-day habit. In fact, if you didn't complete the homework at the end of chapter 8, I'd like you to take out your phone or daily planner right now—go on; I'll wait while you get it—and open up your calendar. Now take a look at your meetings, appointments, and other commitments for the next twenty-one days. Find a window in the morning and a window in the afternoon in which to schedule your Z Technique each day and enter it into your calendar. Set a reminder so that it won't slip your mind, then respect that alert when it pops up. As dear friend of mine, student, and Tony Award–winning actress Laura Benanti says, "I make the appointment with myself and I keep it because I respect myself." Shut your office door, turn off your e-mail alerts, and get this mental hygiene taken care of. You won't ever regret taking the time to meditate.

» Finding the Space to Sit

Do you work in a cubicle or on a sales floor or in any other scenario where you don't have the privacy of an office? Meditate in your car.

Ride the subway instead of driving. Meditate on a bench outside or even in a broom closet. The only thing easier than this style of meditation is finding an excuse not to do any meditation at all—and then you're back where you started or, worse, you're falling behind the pack. You need to set those alarms on your calendar to prompt you until twice a day every day becomes second nature, no matter how busy your day or how busy your mind. In fact, those days when your to-do list just keeps growing or your mind is preoccupied with a million other demands are actually the days when you need the 3 M's more, not less.

There may be times as you are first starting out when you are tempted to skip your regularly scheduled sitting because you feel as if you're just too busy, too tired, or too stressed. *Do it anyway.* Guess what? Oprah is busy, too, but she manages to make time twice every day. When I say this, I often get pushback from people who argue that Oprah has teams of people to delegate responsibilities to, but I always reply by asking which they think came first: the success or the discipline? Saying you're too busy to meditate is like saying you're too busy to stop to get gas for your car; it just doesn't make sense. Do you have time to feel sluggish, stressed, and stupid? Do you have time for your life to grind to a halt while you get sick? Yes, this does require a small investment of time, but the payoff will be exponential: All this takes is 2 percent of your day to drastically improve the other 98 percent. A to-do list that once would have taken you five or six hours might now only take you two or three because your increased energy, reduced stress, and improved intuition are all contributing to increased productivity, accuracy, and creativity. You'll soon find you're not only accomplishing more in less time but are actually accomplishing things at a higher level. Whether it's connecting with clients, innovating in the workplace, managing your family, or simply enjoying the moment-to-moment delights of your daily life, it won't be long before you sense that things are beginning to play out more elegantly and you're stepping into your full performance potential.

» This Is Not a Pedicure for Your Brain

The number one thing I like to tell people who want to lump meditation in with various other luxury items like spa treatments or scented candles is this: *It's not a luxury if it gives you more time.* Luxuries are, by their very definition, indulgences—things that are nice but unnecessary. I firmly believe that after just a few weeks of regular, twice-a-day sittings using the Z Technique, you'll find that the positive results it produces in your mind, body, and professional performance have too significant an impact on your quality of life to be considered a mere luxury. In our fast-paced, highly competitive world, cucumber water and pedicures are luxuries; optimized performance is a necessity.

Remember, however, that "optimized performance" is going to look different for every person. Starting a meditation practice is not going to turn you into a different person with a completely new set of skills and aptitudes. On the surface, it may seem as if we all have the same goals: make more money, free up more time, strengthen our personal relationships, and so on. But the reasons behind those goals are unique for each person. Make more money so you can do what with it? Go hiking in the Andes. Fund research for an alternative to plastic. Buy a house for my mom and dad. Start a ranch for abused horses. Free up more time so you can fill it how? Volunteer in my community. Catch up on all the reading I've always wanted to do. Finally write that book I've talked about for years. Spend more time with my family. Plant that garden I've always wanted. Travel. It's not the money or the time or the relationships we want—it's the feelings those experiences provide. Our ultimate destinations and ambitions are as individual as we are.

Meditation will help you rid your nervous system of the distinct set of stresses you've accumulated throughout your highly individualized lifetime, leaving you better rested, more intuitive, physically healthier, and better able to access energy so you can use your unique expertise to create innovative responses to the specific demands of your life. In short, meditation helps you do you . . . *better*.

Please remember that beginning this journey is not suddenly going to solve all your problems and make you happy 100 percent of the time. Don't let "I'll be happy when . . ." syndrome find a back door into your life by attaching it to meditation. You were happy a million times before you started meditation, and you'll be happy a million times on your journey; your happiness is not dependent on how well you do with this practice. In fact, remember that your first few weeks with the Z Technique may actually bring up old feelings of sadness, anger, fogginess, or fatigue as you bravely move through the initial emotional and physical detox. But remember: "Better out than in." For real. This stuff can either get cried out into your tissues or stuck in your *physical* tissues, where they may manifest into sickness and disease over time. So choose activities that will help you move this old stress up and out, without taking it out on your nearest and dearest. I want to repeat this for emphasis. As you start your daily practice, you might notice a lifetime of old stress coming up and out. This might feel intense and you might not like it. It might even be confusing if you skipped chapter 3 and have no idea what I am talking about and expect to be floating on a cloud of bliss from day one. The Z Technique will not make you numb or immune to feelings. Think of it more like a purge, and the more deliberate you are about scheduling activities that help you move things up and out, the easier it will be to not take them out on your partner, roommate, dog, or local barista. While this purge might not be what you were expecting or hoping for when you picked up this book, take comfort in knowing that it is the very thing that creates more mental space for heightened performance.

As you move through this unstressing period, there is an advanced technique I sometimes share with my more experienced students to use a few minutes after their practice to reframe events from their pasts. I invite them to reflect on a particularly difficult or trying period in their lives and see it through the lens they have now. Knowing that everything is working out exactly as meant, they comfort or encourage this younger version of themselves by communicating anything that would bring strength. I am obviously not suggesting meditation as a kind of time travel, but simply that this subtler state of consciousness can impact your perception and experience of time, and taking a few minutes to revisit important events from your past from your least excited state of awareness can help you answer the question "Why did that happen *for* me?" Did it help you gain new perspective? Did it make you stronger? Did it prepare you for a future job? In a roundabout way, was it the first step on the journey that led you to where you are today? By looking at how your past challenges set you on the course to your present circumstances, you might up-level your *perception* of and attitude toward the past and finally be able to release any stress attached to it once and for all. This isn't magic. It takes commitment to do every day, twice a day.

There is an old story that meditation teachers often share about the way monks in the Himalayas dye their saffron-yellow robes. The fabric doesn't get that bright on the first dip in the vat of dye, or the second, or the third. It has to be immersed over and over again until it achieves its distinctive hue. The fabric can't just be dropped in the vat and left to soak for weeks on end, either; it must be soaked in the dye until it is saturated and then placed in the sun to dry. Otherwise, it mildews. Conversely, it can't be left in the sun too long, because it can become faded and brittle. Instead, the fabric must be moved back and forth, from the dye to the sun, sun to dye, countless times before it becomes totally colorfast. Then no amount of sun or wear will change the colorfastness of this cloth.

Meditation is doing this for our bodies! It is making us colorfast with bliss. But the timing matters and consistency matters. There is no need to meditate for hours and hours or days and days on end. That would be the equivalent of sitting in the dye for too long. After fifteen minutes, we're saturated. Similarly we don't want to go days or weeks without meditating. That would be the equivalent of drying in the sun for too long.

What we do instead is wake up and flood our bodies and brains with bliss and fulfillment in the vat of meditation, then we dry out on the demands of our day. In midafternoon, we dip back in the dye, and then dry out on the demands of the evening and night. We go to sleep and do the whole thing over again the next day. This cycle of meditation and activity—saturating the nervous system with dopamine and serotonin, and then drying out on the demands of our day—is the very thing that ushers us into higher states of performance.

What I love about this story is that it illustrates that the goal of meditation is not to eliminate your demands; *your demands are not keeping you from enlightenment.* Neither is the goal of this technique to just luxuriate in the bliss field all day while the rest of the world continues to tick away around you. You need to have both the dyeing and the drying, the meditation and the activity. It is in the constant meeting of the two—the demands and the fulfillment you deliver to them, the sun and the dye—that you achieve the most elegant version of you.

Inspired to Learn More?

Do you want to be personally guided through your meditation journey?

For guided visualizations and audio versions of some of the exercises in this book, visit www.zivameditation.com/bookbonus.

You can learn the full Ziva Technique through our fifteen-day online training, zivaONLINE. Visit www.zivameditation.com /online.

To join our global community of Ziva Meditators and get your meditation questions answered, request access to our Facebook group, zivaTRIBE, at www.facebook.com/groups/zivaTRIBE/.

» About Ziva Meditation

» www.zivameditation.com

Ziva is a school for high performance. We are all about giving people tools to perform at the top of their personal and professional game.

Over twenty-five hundred students have learned the Ziva Technique with us in person, and over nine thousand people around the world have learned from zivaONLINE. All of them have graduated with a powerful practice to take with them for life. The Ziva

Technique is a trifecta of mindfulness, meditation, and manifesting. We are partnering with some of the world's leading neuroscientists and creators of body-tracking technology to make ancient tools accessible and easy to adopt into your fast-paced life.

Ziva graduates include winners of the Oscar, Grammy, Emmy, Golden Globe, and Tony awards, as well as CEOs, NBA players, Navy SEALs, military veterans, entrepreneurs, and full-time parents. Ziva is based in New York City, where we offer our in-person training, zivaLIVE, once a month; courses in LA are offered several times per year. Corporate and private courses can be customized to your needs. This practice can revolutionize how you work, live, and love.

Acknowledgments

What a joy to have a few pages to publicly thank the incredible tribe of humans (and my dog, Mugsy) who have collaborated, created, and sacrificed to make this book possible. Thank you for reading these words and for sending them some love.

First of all, to every person who has trusted me enough to introduce them to these powerful tools, thank you. Thank you for being my best teachers, thank you for laughing at my jokes that were actually funny, and thank you for staring silently at the jokes that weren't so I would know what to include in this book and what to leave out. A special shout-out to those of you brave enough to share your stories, your challenges, and your successes in this book. Reading the in-depth transformations that have occurred for you due to your commitment to the practice was the most inspiring part of this process.

To my ridiculously smart and funny husband, Jason: I could write an entire book on the wisdom I have gained from you. Thank you for your curiosity, for your integrity, for leading by example, and for patiently waiting for dinner while I spent "just one more hour" on the manuscript. Most important, thank you for seeing me, for helping me prioritize, and for challenging me to step into my full potential. I love you.

To Cassie Hanjian, thank you for coming to me with the original idea for this book so many years ago. Thanks for taking my first Ziva course in the basement of that dingy gym, for reading the article in the *New York Times,* and for trusting your gut that the world is ready for a book about meditation for extraordinary performance. You have truly been the midwife for this project. Thank you for wrangling my ideas and bringing me back to the core message again and again. Thank you for holding my hand and teaching me how to be a writer. This book would not have been even a twinkle in my eye without you.

To Tiffany Yecke Brooks. You are a full-blown rock star of a writer and editor. Thank you for helping me shape and craft these ideas so they translate to the page. Thank you for your endless enthusiasm, for sitting through the Ziva course so many times, and for sharing your unique gifts with me and everyone who reads these words. I am forever grateful.

To the now infamous "Australian woman sitting next to me in the dressing room," Deonne Zanotto. If you hadn't been so damn good at your job and performed so well under pressure, I might never have gotten over my preconceived notions about meditation. Thank you for shining so brightly that you inspired me to take up this habit in the first place.

To Michael Miller, thank you for planting the first seed of meditation in my oh-so-stressy brain. Who knew that seed would grow into something that would plant so many more?

Without fertile soil, no seed can grow. To my mom, Margie Fletcher, and sister, Jessica Fletcher, your lifetime of love and support have nourished me into believing I can accomplish anything I want. I love you.

John Hastings, thank you for helping create the organization and structure that would become *Stress Less, Accomplish More.* John Lynn, you are a dream of a father-in-law. Your steady counsel has allowed me the space and time I needed to write this.

Surrounding yourself with people who inspire you may be the single biggest life lesson I will pass on to my son. To call the following people *friends* is an honor I do not take lightly. Thank you to each of you for your commitment to making this world a healthier, happier, and more hospitable place to live. Thank you for championing me and sharing Ziva with your audiences, and thank you for playing big and inspiring me to do the same: JJ Virgin, Dr. Mark Hyman, Dave Asprey, Andrew Huberman, and Vishen Lakhiani—it all started in Greece, and I am excited to see how far things can go.

Cassie Jones, what an honor to publish this with you. I knew from our very first meeting that you get it. Thank you for taking a gamble on a first-time writer and for believing in the scope and magnitude of what this practice can do for the country and the world.

To the ever-inspiring zivaTEAM, Laura Sills, Sherri Kronfeld, Elizabeth Joyce Korfmacher, Ali McCabe, Liza Fernandez, Whitney Diamond, Zara Louy, Lauren Shaw, and Thomas Kavanagh: There are not enough words to express my gratitude for all that you do to make Ziva run so elegantly. It is your intelligence, hard work, and compassion that really make the company special and allow our students to thrive.

To Ashley Chappell, Abra Williams, Sarah Yargrouh, Heather Weiss, Radha Agrawal, and Sandy Kenyon, thank you for your endless enthusiasm and desire to get the message of this book to the masses. Without you this book would not have had nearly the impact I know it is capable of.

To my dog, Mugsy, you have done absolutely nothing to help make this book a reality. Your over-the-top cuteness did nothing but distract me and slow me down. You have, however, expanded my capacity for love—which I hope every reader feels in the pages of this book.

And finally, to my soon-to-be-born son, you have been a real trouper in utero. You have made this pregnancy a delight. You have sacrificed a decent amount of sleep while your mom continued to teach and write. Thanks for not sucking *all* my energy and for allowing me to have some creativity left to put these words on the page. At the end of the day, my real intention is that you grow up in a world where people take responsibility for cleaning their own emotional house instead of taking it out on others; a world where it's more common to take a meditation break than a coffee break, and where people take better care of each other because they have a tool to help them feel, on a visceral level, that there really is only one thing . . . and we are all it.

Notes

Chapter 2: Tapping the Source

1. J. David Creswell et al., "Alterations in Resting-State Functional Connectivity Link Mindfulness Meditation with Reduced Interleukin-6: A Randomized Controlled Trial." *Biological Psychiatry Journal* 80, no. 1 (July 2016): 53–61.

2. David Gelles, "At Aetna, a C.E.O.'s Management by Mantra," *New York Times*, February 27, 2015, https://www.nytimes.com/2015/03/01/business/at-aetna-a-ceos-management-by-mantra.html.

Chapter 3: Stress Makes You Stupid

1. David Yamada, "Is Stress the 'Black Plague' of the 21st Century?" *New Workplace Institute Blog*, last modified November 18, 2010, accessed August 25, 2017, https://newworkplace.wordpress.com/2010/11/18/is-stress-the-black-plague-of-the-21st-century/.

2. Eileen Luders et al., "Bridging the Hemispheres in Meditation: Thicker Callosal Regions and Enhanced Fractional Anisotropy (FA) in Long-Term Practitioners," *Neuroimage* 61, no. 1 (May 15, 2012): 181–87, https://www.ncbi.nlm.nih.gov/pubmed/22374478.

3. Brigid Schulte, "Harvard Neuroscientist: Meditation Not Only Reduces Stress, Here's How It Changes Your Brain," *Washington Post*, May 26, 2015, https://www.washingtonpost.com/news/inspired-life

/wp/2015/05/26/harvard-neuroscientist-meditation-not-only-reduces
-stress-it-literally-changes-your-brain/?utm_term=.03139d47d453.

4.   Melanie Curtin, "Want to Raise Your IQ by 23 Percent? Neuroscience
        Says Take Up This Simple Habit," *Inc.*, last modified December 1, 2016,
        accessed November 12, 2017, https://www.inc.com/melanie-curtin
        /want-to-raise-your-iq-by-23-percent-neuroscience-says-to-take-up
        -this-simple-hab.html.

Chapter 4: Sleepless in Seattle—and Everywhere Else

1.   Farrell Cahill, "Sleep Deprivation: As Damaging to Brain Health as
        Binge Drinking?" *Brain Health* (blog), last modified July 11, 2017, ac-
        cessed on October 3, 2017, https://blog.medisys.ca/sleep-deprivation
        -as-damaging-to-brain-health-as-binge-drinking.

2.   Helen Anderson, "The Effects of Caffeine on Adenosine," Livestrong
        .com, last modified October 3, 2017, accessed on October 6, 2017, https://
        www.livestrong.com/article/481979-the-effects-of-caffeine-on-adenosine/.

Chapter 5: Sick of Being Sick

1.   Damian H. Gilling et al., "Antiviral Efficacy and Mechanisms of Action
        of Oregano Essential Oil and Its Primary Component Carvacrol Against
        Murine Norovirus," *Journal of Applied Microbiology* 116, no. 5 (May
        2014): 1149–63, https://www.ncbi.nlm.nih.gov/pubmed/24779581.

2.   Fadel Zeidan et al., "Mindfulness Meditation Trumps Placebo in Pain
        Reduction," WakeHealth.edu, accessed January 28, 2018, http://www
        .wakehealth.edu/News-Releases/2015/Mindfulness_Meditation
        _Trumps_Placebo_in_Pain_Reduction.htm.

Chapter 6: The (Legit) Fountain of Youth

1.   Isha Sadhguru, "Are There Choices about Death?" *Isha* (blog), accessed
        January 22, 2018, http://isha.sadhguru.org/blog/yoga-meditation
        /demystifying-yoga/are-there-choices-about-death/.

2.   Anne E. Moyer et al., "Stress-induced Cortisol Response and Fat Distribution in Women," *Obesity Research* 2, no. 3 (May 1994): 255–62, https://www.ncbi.nlm.nih.gov/pubmed/16353426.

3.   Britta Hölzel et al., "Mindfulness Practice Leads to Increases in Regional Brain Gray Matter Density," *Psychiatry Research: Neuroimaging* 191, no. 1 (January 30, 2011): 36–43, https://www.sciencedirect.com/science/article/pii/S092549271000288X.

4.   Elissa S. Epel et al., "Accelerated Telomere Shortening in Response to Life Stress," *Proceedings of the National Academy of Sciences of the United States* 101, no. 49 (December 7, 2004): 17312–15, https://www.ncbi.nlm.nih.gov/pubmed/15574496.

5.   Elissa S. Epel et al., "Can Meditation Slow Rate of Cellular Aging? Cognitive Stress, Mindfulness, and Telomeres," *Annals of the New York Academy of Sciences* 1172 (August 2009): 34–53, https://www.ncbi.nlm.nih.gov/pubmed/19735238.

6.   Elizabeth A. Hoge et al., "Loving-Kindness Meditation Practice Associated with Longer Telomeres in Women," *Brain, Behavior, and Immunity* 32 (August 2013): 159–63.

7.   Eileen Luders, Nicolas Cherbuin, and Florian Kuth, "Forever Young(er): Potential Age-Defying Effects of Long-Term Meditation on Gray Matter Atrophy," *Frontiers in Psychology* 5 (January 21, 2015), https://doi.org/10.3389/fpsyg.2014.01551.

Chapter 7: The "I'll Be Happy When . . ." Syndrome

1.   Phil. 4:7.

Chapter 8: The Z Technique

1.   Alex Korb, *The Upward Spiral: Using Neuroscience to Reverse the Course of Depression, One Small Change at a Time* (Oakland, CA: New Harbinger Publications, 2015).

Chapter 9: Better Parking Karma

1. David DeDesteno, "The Kindness Cure," *The Atlantic,* July 21, 2015, https://www.TheAtlantic.com/Health/Archive/E/2015/07/Mindfulness -Meditation-Empathy-Compassion/398867/.

Chapter 10: The Most Amazing Version of You

1. Tesla Memorial Society of New York, "Nikola Tesla and Swami Vivekananda," accessed September 22, 2017, http://www.teslasociety .com/tesla_and_swami.htm.

2. Srini Pillay, *Tinker Dabble Doodle Try: Unlock the Power of the Unfocused Mind* (New York: Ballantine Books, 2017).

3. Creswell et al., "Alterations in Resting-State Functional Connectivity."

4. Andrew C. Hafenbrack, Zoe Kinias, and Sigal G. Barsade, "Debiasing the Mind Through Meditation: Mindfulness and the Sunk-Cost Bias," *Psychological Science* 25, no. 2 (February 1, 2014): 369–76.

Chapter 11: From Om to OMG!

1. Robin Caryn Rabin, "Sleep: Study Finds Many Are Too Tired for Sex," *New York Times,* March 8, 2010, http://www.nytimes.com/2010/03/09 /health/research/09beha.html.

2. Lisa Dawn Hamilton, Alessandra H. Rellini, and Cindy M. Metson, "Cortisol, Sexual Arousal, and Affect in Response to Sexual Stimuli," *Journal of Sexual Medicine* 5, no. 9 (September 2008): 2111–18, http:// www.jsm.jsexmed.org/article/S1743-6095(15)32148-2/fulltext.

3. Julie Marks, "Erectile Dysfunction: Symptoms and Causes," Everyday Health, last modified December 20, 2017, accessed November 1, 2017, https://www.everydayhealth.com/erectile-dysfunction/guide/#01.

4. Troels W. Kjaer et al., "Increased Dopamine Tone During Meditation-Induced Change of Consciousness," *Cognitive Brain Research* 13, no. 2 (April 2002): 255–59, https://www.sciencedirect.com/journal/cognitive -brain-research.

5.   Vilayanur Ramachandran, "Mirror Neurons and Imitation Learning as the Driving Force Behind the Great Leap Forward in Human Evolution," Edge, last modified May 31, 2000, accessed November 15, 2017, https://www.edge.org/conversation/mirror-neurons-and-imitation -learning-as-the-driving-force-behind-the-great-leap-forward-in-human -evolution.

Index

About Emily Fletcher

Emily Fletcher is the founder of Ziva and the creator of the Ziva Technique. She is regarded as the leading expert in meditation for high performance.

The *New York Times*, the *Today* show, *Vogue*, and ABC News have all featured Emily's work. She's been named one of the top one hundred women in wellness to watch by MindBodyGreen; has taught more than fifteen thousand students around the world; and has spoken on meditation for performance at Google, Harvard Business School, Summit Series, Viacom, Wanderlust Festival, and the Omega Center. Ziva graduates include Oscar-, Grammy-, Emmy-, and Tony-award winners, as well as NBA players, CEOs, busy parents, entrepreneurs, and everyone in between.

Her recent accomplishments provide a stark contrast to the stressed-out Broadway performer she was ten years ago. During Emily's career on Broadway, which included roles in *Chicago*, *The Producers*, and *A Chorus Line*, she began going gray at age twenty-seven, suffering from insomnia, underperforming at work, and getting sick four to five times a year—and believing this was all "normal."

In 2008, Emily was introduced to a powerful practice that cured her eighteen-month battle with insomnia on the very first day. She stopped going gray, she stopped getting sick, and she started kicking ass at work (and loving it). Her physical and professional transformation was so dramatic that she felt inspired to share it with others.

One year later, Emily left Broadway for Rishikesh, India, to begin what would become three years of teacher training. She founded Ziva in 2011, with the opening of the New York City studio, and created the world's first online meditation training program.

After years of teaching thousands of people, Emily realized that meditation was not enough to help her students perform at the top of their personal and professional game. In 2017, Emily developed the Ziva Technique: a powerful trifecta of Mindfulness, Meditation, and Manifesting designed to unlock your full potential. The proven benefits of the Ziva Technique include decreased stress, less anxiety, deeper sleep, improved immune function, increased productivity, and extraordinary performance.

Emily's teaching style is entertaining, accessible, easy to adopt, and attracts many top performers from around the globe.

You can enroll in zivaONLINE or zivaLIVE courses at www.zivameditation.com.